Slavenka Drakulić, born in Croatia in 1949, is a writer
and journalist whose four previous novels (*The Taste of a
Man*, *Holograms of Fear*, *Marble Skin* and *As If I Am Not
There*) and three non-fiction books (*How We Survived
Communism and Even Laughed*, *Balkan Express* and
Café Europa) have been translated into many major
European languages. She contributes to *Süddeutsche
Zeitung*, *La Stampa* and *Dagens Nyheter*, and her
writing has appeared in magazines and newspapers
around the world. She writes both in Croatian and
English.

Also by Slavenka Drakulić

They Would Never Hurt a Fly

War Criminals on Trial in The Hague

SLAVENKA DRAKULIĆ

An *Abacus* Original

First published in Great Britain by Abacus in 2004

A CIP catalogue record for this book
is available from the British Library.

ISBN 0 349 11775 6

Typeset in Stempel Garamond by M Rules
Printed and bound in Great Britain by
Clays Ltd, St Ives plc

Abacus
An imprint of
Time Warner Book Group UK
Brettenham House
Lancaster Place
London WC2E 7EN

www.TimeWarnerBooks.co.uk

CONTENTS

He has driven the dichotomy of private and public functions, of family and occupation, so far that he can no longer find in his own person any connection between the two. When his occupation forces him to murder people he does not regard himself as a murderer because he has not done it out of inclination but in his professional capacity. Out of sheer passion he would never do harm to a fly.

Hannah Arendt, *Essays in Understanding 1930–1954*

They Would Never
Hurt a Fly

INTRODUCTION

Not a Fairy Tale

Once upon a time, in a faraway part of Europe, behind seven mountains and seven seas, there was a beautiful country called Yugoslavia. Its people belonged to six different nationalities, were of three different religions and spoke three different languages. They were Croats, Serbs, Slovenes, Albanians, Bosnians and Macedonians, yet they all worked together, went to school together, married each other and lived in relative harmony for forty-five years.

But because it is not a fairy tale the story of this beautiful country has no happy ending. Yugoslavia fell apart in a terrible and bloody war, a war that claimed some two hundred thousand lives – mostly in Bosnia – displaced two million people and produced several new states: Slovenia, Bosnia, Croatia, Serbia and Macedonia. Albanians and Montenegrins are still struggling for their independence.

This all happened in the middle of Europe not so long ago, between 1991 and 1995. The whole world was surprised by this war. We, the citizens of Yugoslavia, were even more surprised. When I think about it, I am still angry with myself.

Is it possible that the war crept into our lives slowly, stealthily, like a thief? Why didn't we see it coming? Why didn't we do something to prevent it? Why were we so arrogant that we thought it could not happen to us? Were we really prisoners of a fairy tale?

My generation in Europe grew up believing that, after the Second World War, a similar conflict could not happen again. Nuclear war between two superpowers was a possibility, but not a local one fought with conventional weapons. Another argument against the likelihood of a new war was the fact that in the Second World War in Yugoslavia hundreds of thousands perished on all sides. The witnesses were still alive, the wounds were still open. And, finally, we knew that Yugoslavia had no enemies. We lived peacefully with our neighbours: with Italians, Austrians, Hungarians, Romanians, Bulgarians and Albanians.

But one day we discovered that it is not necessary to have an outside enemy to start a war. The enemy could be inside – and indeed it was. It was bad enough digging up the past – the past that we tend to forget, the fact that during the war Yugoslavia was occupied or controlled by Nazi Germany – but there was also a civil war between Serbs and Croats going on. In other words, there was a recorded history of bloodshed in our country, and it was easy to manipulate it in order to antagonise one another: Serbs became the enemies of Croats, Bosnian Muslims and Albanians, but at one point Croats were also at war not only with Serbs, but with Muslims as well, while Macedonians' enemies were Albanians.

Even if it appeared so to us, the war, however, did not descend upon us overnight. In the late eighties communism collapsed everywhere in Eastern Europe and in what was then still the Soviet Union. Yugoslavia was unprepared for the political changes that followed that collapse. We had not developed any democratic alternatives as Poland and Czechoslovakia had done, and the political vacuum was suddenly filled with nationalist parties. They all had the same programme: independence and nation-states of their own.

Simmering nationalism was soon spreading like a fire. The nationalist parties were voted into power in Croatia and Bosnia. In Serbia something strange happened: the Communist Party turned nationalist, led by Slobodan Milošević, who believed this was the way to keep his grip on power. Soon there were referendums all over the country, and people were voting for their independence from Yugoslavia. Slovenia took the first step, and by June 1991 it was out of the federation. The break-up had begun. The Jugoslavenska Narodna Armija (Yugoslav National Army) tried to stop Slovenia from leaving, but, as it had no minorities to speak of, the army let it go.

At this point, war still did not look like a possibility. The names of the few soldiers and policemen killed during that spring of 1991 in Slovenia and Croatia were still noticed. Their deaths were still exceptional, and their photographs and names were printed on the front pages of newspapers.

But Croatia had a large Serbian minority, and Slobodan Milošević, as President of Serbia, had the perfect excuse to send his army to 'protect' the Serbs there. That meant real war. In the autumn of 1991, the Croatian town of Vukovar was almost erased from the face of the earth, and some ten thousand people lost their lives. In the years that followed, death became an ordinary thing and nobody bothered to list the victims' names any more. It was too late for that.

In Bosnia, where Serbs, Croats and Muslims lived together, the war started in April 1992. Because of the mixed population, it also took on the characteristics of a civil war. The Serbian minority there, 'protected' by Milošević, proclaimed the independent state of Republika Srpska. Not being able to prevent either Croatia or Bosnia from leaving Yugoslavia, Milošević – together with Serbs from Republika Srpska – now embarked on the war for a 'Great Serbia'. The two-year siege of Sarajevo followed, and a couple of years later the UN-protected Muslim enclave of Srebrenica fell to the army of Republika Srpska. Some seven thousand unarmed Muslim men were executed – the largest massacre in Europe since 1945.

As these newly created states at war – Bosnia, Croatia, Republika Srpska, Serbia – were led by hard-core nationalist leaders, it was soon clear that they were fighting not only for independence, but also for 'ethnically cleansed' nation-states. Entire regions in Croatia and Bosnia – and, later on, in Kosovo as well – were 'ethnically cleansed' (a euphemism that in practice often meant genocide) in order to achieve a homogeneous population, not unlike Hitler's Germany of *'Ein Reich, ein Volk, ein Führer'*. Both Serbs and Croats wanted to carve up Bosnia between themselves, leaving only small enclaves to the Muslims.

The war in Bosnia ended with the Dayton Agreement in November 1995, but it was not yet finished in Kosovo, a southern province of Serbia populated mainly by Albanians. They, too, wanted independence and began to fight for it. Milošević's retaliation was such that at one point hundreds of thousands of Albanians left their homes in panic in order to avoid being killed, and tried to cross the border into Albania or Macedonia. With at least seven hundred thousand refugees leaving Kosovo, it was a humanitarian disaster. At that point, in the spring of 1999, NATO decided to bomb Milošević into submission.

This was the beginning of the end of Slobodan Milošević. In October 2000 the unimaginable happened: Milošević lost the elections – and his power. He was soon arrested and then delivered to the International Criminal Tribunal for the former Yugoslavia (ICTY) in The Hague. This Tribunal had been formed in 1993 in the Netherlands, after the international community realised that the new states that had come out of the war were unable or unwilling to prosecute their war criminals themselves. As stated at the Tribunal, all sides committed war crimes, but Serbia committed most of them. Arresting and extraditing war criminals became the biggest political issue in Croatia, Serbia and Bosnia, where persons now listed in The Hague as war criminals were hailed as national heroes at home.

Today there are some eighty people being prosecuted at the Tribunal, from all sides at war. My choice of characters in this book is a personal, not a representative, one. My interest is not only centred on the most important alleged war criminals like Slobodan Milošević, but also on those whose cases or personalities I found relevant to the purpose of this book, regardless of their nationality. The fact that there are no Muslim war criminals described at any length in this book is therefore just a coincidence; it certainly doesn't mean that they did not commit crimes of that type. You can see their names on the ICTY list of wanted men. I also describe two people who have not been on trial at the Tribunal, but who are nevertheless important for understanding the issues at hand. One is a witness, Milan Levar, and the other is Slobodan Milošević's wife, Mirjana Mira Marković.

My interest in writing this book was a simple one: as it cannot be denied that war crimes were committed, I wanted to find out about the people who committed them. Who were they? Ordinary people like you or me – or monsters?

And to answer the question I originally raised: why didn't we see war coming? Certainly we could see the writing on the wall. There were many signs of the coming disaster, yet we were not capable of reading them properly until it was too late. But it is easy to be wise in hindsight. Could the war have been prevented? Perhaps. But too few people tried to do it.

1

Why The Hague?

For some time after the war in Croatia was over – although in Bosnia it was still in progress – a young man who was a friend of my daughter stayed in our house in Zagreb. I noticed that he never switched off the light in his room at night. When I asked him why, he told me, briefly. He might wake up during the night not knowing where he was. He might have bad dreams – dreams about his friends, soldiers who disappeared in action in Bosnia, and very probably were killed. But he would say no more than this.

Now he has a family and a baby daughter, and I am sure he will never tell her about his friends. But if she does grow up hearing his stories about the war in Bosnia, she will be confused. At school, she will probably learn that, officially, Croatia was never at war with Bosnia, was never an aggressor. Officially, her father was not fighting Muslims in Bosnia, and his friends were not killed there either. If the history books of today are any indication, the girl may be taught that the 'war for the Homeland', as it is called, was a defensive war and nothing more. Moreover, because it was a defensive war,

Croatian soldiers could not have committed war crimes. At least, this has been the official doctrine in Croatia for the last ten years, and it did not change with the death of the first Croatian president, Franjo Tudjman, in 1999.

A girl in Serbia will probably also grow up amidst denial about the war. If she should ask her father about the war in Croatia or in Bosnia, he might reply: War? What war? The only wars Serbs recognise are the NATO war against them and their own war against 'terrorism' in Kosovo. The wars in Croatia and Bosnia do not count for them.

This is how I imagine my father must have felt after the war in 1945: exactly like my daughter's friend. I don't know if he kept the light on in his room, but my father was twenty-three and wanted to forget all the terrible experiences he had had during the five years of war. The bad times were behind him. Soon he met my mother, and they started a family. I was born in 1949. The future looked bright.

My father never spoke about the four years he fought as a partisan under the command of Josip Broz Tito in the Second World War. He wanted to forget it, and for a long time I saw this as a sign of sanity and self-preservation. 'A human being survives by his ability to forget,' Varlam Shalamov writes in *Kolyma Tales*. But I know that, even though he did not speak about it, my father must have remembered the war. It was the single most important period in his life, and he must have been marked by it much more than I have been marked by the recent war in the former Yugoslavia. He fought; I did not. And the more I think about it, the more I am convinced that the combination of his silence and the official version of the historical events of 1939–45 made this latest war possible.

Although my father did not talk about what he saw or experienced, there are three images that I, as a child, used to connect with that war – with his war. The first image comes from my grandmother. She also spent the war with the partisan army, cooking and washing for them, and she often recounted an episode from that time that was fixed in her memory. The partisans had recaptured a Croatian village that had been held earlier by Serbian Chetniks. The village was empty now, the people had fled. As my grandmother entered a deserted house she planned to stay in overnight, she noticed a strange smell. It was a smell of burned meat. The Chetniks had left in haste, and she was convinced there was some food burning on the stove. But there was no food there. She opened the oven. Inside it she found a newborn child roasted like a piglet.

When I was small, I used to imagine my grandma entering that house. I could sense that strange smell, even if I had never smelled it. In my mind I could see a black iron stove fed by logs in front of me, and her hand opening it. I could imagine her horror, too. In time, her horror became mine.

The second image stuck in my mind is one I saw in a movie entitled *Kozara*, but it was real to me. I was thirteen. I remember well the fear I felt while I watched it, my per-spiration, sweaty palms, tears. It was one of those obligatory movies about Tito's partisan battles with the German Army that our history teacher took us to see. There is a scene in which the hero – a partisan, of course – is hiding in a hole in the ground. German soldiers are looking for him. They are coming closer and closer. He can hear them shouting. In his arms he holds a small child and, as the enemy soldiers approach, the child starts crying. The hero closes the baby's mouth with one hand. With the other hand he holds up the makeshift roof of the hole. In the most breathtaking moment of the film a German soldier is stabbing at the earth with his bayonet, trying to find the hero's hiding place, and he cuts through the palm of the hero's hand.

My third image of the war comes from a book that my father tried to keep away from us children, but I managed to get hold of it anyway. It would have been better if I had not, because I could not ask Father about what I saw in it, and it took me a long time to understand what the frightening images in the book were about. I remember it quite distinctly. It was a slim volume of yellowish paper with a green cloth cover. Inside there were a few black and white photographs. They were of poor quality, not very clear. But they were clear enough for me to be able to make out emaciated people sitting or lying on bunk beds, naked skeletons and heaps of corpses on the ground. The title of the book was *Jasenovac*. Years later, when I visited the museum of the concentration camp near Jasenovac, I saw the same pictures. I also saw a collection of knives and hammers that the Ustashe, Croatian fascists, used to kill some seventy thousand people. Twenty thousand of them were Jews; the others were Serbs, gypsies and Croatian communists.

We grew up with many such images, gathered from movies, literature and family stories. On the one hand we had memory, but on the other we had our history books, which shaped history to suit the Communist Party ideology. It was not that we were sheltered from the past. On the contrary, we may have had too much of it. But our history books were filled not with facts but with legends: with Tito's army offensives, his great battles and his even greater victories. Decades later, when I learned about the great massacre that had taken place in the spring of 1945 near Bleiburg in Austria, where tens of thousands of soldiers of the fascist Independent State of Croatia, in retreat and considering surrendering to the Allies, were killed mercilessly by Tito's antifascist army, it was too late to recondition me. I already had a very clear idea that partisans were antifascist heroes, the very opposite of Chetniks,

Germans and Ustashe. At that point, no historical facts that I learned about with astonishment later on could erase these pictures from my early childhood memory about who were the good guys and who were the bad. It must have been the same for people whose uncles or fathers were killed there by partisans. They, too, grew up with memories of these relatives while knowing that their slaughter was not even mentioned in the history books. My generation grew up never learning history – history as we knew it was a lie, a deceit.

Only now can I understand how easy it is to start a war in the absence of facts. War does not come from nowhere; I saw in Yugoslavia that it must be prepared. It is easy for political leaders to use images like the ones that I remember, to use people's emotional memory and build hatred upon it. Because in totalitarian societies, where there is no true history, each person has in his own memory a collection of such images, and it becomes dangerous if he has nothing more than that. Political leaders can appeal to these images, mix them with popular mythology and stir emotions by repeating propaganda endlessly on television. One can hardly defend oneself against such propaganda if there is no common history that everybody can believe in. A thin layer of rationality easily falls away under the pressure of emotions. The history we learned – which was not in fact history at all – made it easier for us to abandon reason in favour of pure emotions.

So when I experienced the same silence, the same absence of a desire for truth and the same kind of manipulation of facts after the end of the war in 1995, I became afraid. This was the third time I had been confronted with the 'point zero' of history. First it had happened with my father's generation after the Second World War, that is, after the communist revolution. All history before then was rewritten. The second time it happened was after the collapse of communism, when we had to forget about communism and begin again (and start rewriting history again) from the year 1990. And the third time is now, the present, following the end of the last war. In Croatia it is easy to perceive the general unwillingness to talk about the war at all, almost as if it never happened. It is even easier to conclude that people are tired of it and want to leave the past behind and think of the future. After all, thinking of the past got them into the war in the first place. Politicians are all too happy to join the majority of the people and preach the message of 'turning a new page of history' – a blank one, if possible – because many of them are still in power and don't want to accept the responsibility for a past war.

Yet, if the truth is not established about the so-called 'war for the Homeland', the next generation will one day find themselves in exactly the same situation as my post-Second World War generation. All they will have to rely upon will be dusty images and bloody stories. These will vary, depending on which side their parents were on, but they will be left with only memory, not history.

But the war is still with us. One need only mention The Hague to see that. I imagine that every Dutchman would be astonished by the strong emotions provoked in Croatia, Serbia and even Bosnia (because Bosnia is more cooperative with the Tribunal) by the mention of this pretty Dutch city. Ever since 1993, when the International Criminal Tribunal for the former Yugoslavia was established there, The Hague has been a source of controversy in the Balkans. The ICTY was established because former Yugoslav states were either unable or unwilling to prosecute their own war criminals. Far from being independent, their judicial systems were deeply corrupt, and there would have been enormous political pressure if alleged war criminals were tried in local courts. Back home in Croatia, this argument immediately became fiercely disputed. Opponents of the International Tribunal from the right argued that the ICTY court was a political instrument established to punish and humiliate their country. The more sophisticated critics argued that it would be better to hold the trials for war criminals at home, because it would give the nation a way to face the truth about the war and experience a catharsis.

I was naive enough to believe that one of the priorities of the new post-Tudjman government would be to try to face the truth about the war: why did it happen? What was it about? Did the Croatian Army commit war crimes or not? It is, of course, a hard truth: the war was about forming a nation-state, which involved 'ethnic cleansing'; two hundred thousand Serbs were forced to leave Krajina; their homes were burned and plundered; some four hundred civilians were killed; Serb civilians in Gospić, Pakrac or Sisak were executed en masse; twenty-four thousand Muslims were detained by Bosnian Croatian soldiers in forty-four concentration camps in Herzegovina; Croats killed 116 civilians in the village of Ahmici and blew up the old bridge in Mostar; in 1991, in Zagreb, a twelve-year-old girl named Aleksandra Zec was killed, along with her Serbian parents. Her murderer, who confessed, is still at large.

However, nobody wants to speak this truth out loud. Nor does anybody want to hear it, for that matter. This is because in Croatia the truth is dangerous. For ten years Tudjman's propaganda convinced Croats that people on the Tribunal's list of war criminals – like Mladen Naletilić Tuta, Tihomir Blaškić, Dario Kordić, Mirko Norac and Ante Gotovina – should be seen as heroes. If Tudjman's government extradited them, it was only because of serious international pressure, not because Croats believed they should be tried. But how is it possible for the views from both inside and outside to be so conflicting? It is possible because Croats were never told that these men were 'willing executioners', even if they were war heroes. So when these men are suspected by The Hague of either committing or ordering the killing of civilians, Croats become offended. Their heroes war criminals? Never! To stand up against the Tribunal became a sign of patriotism. The opponents of the Tribunal claim that the Tribunal is trying not individuals but the whole of Croatia for war crimes. When, in the spring of 2001, Mirko Norac was ordered to appear in a local court in Rijeka on suspicion of committing war crimes in Gospić, where over a hundred Serbs had disappeared in the autumn of 1991, war veterans organised a protest rally in Split. Some seventy-five thousand people attended that rally. The government was in crisis and the whole country paralysed for at least a week.

Establishing the truth about the war is at the heart of the controversies surrounding The Hague Tribunal. Until the truth about the war is established, trials of the war criminals, whether in the International Tribunal or in the local courts, will be seen as an injustice to the 'war heroes'. There is no justice without truth, and Croatia is still far from such truth. Recently two trials of war criminals took place: one of the 'Gospić group' in Rijeka and the other of a group of prison guards in Split. The trial in Split in particular has degenerated into a shameful performance with the public applauding their 'heroes' while threatening the witnesses. The judge released the defendants from prison, but a higher court reversed the decision – only to discover that two defendants had escaped in the meantime. Witnesses in both trials have been prone to sudden losses of memory. Or in the case of Sisak, a small town near Zagreb where, during 1991 and 1992, a large number of Serbian civilians disappeared, a local judge ordered an investigation ten years after the event, and then only under pressure from the media, especially the magazine *Hrvatska ljevica,* which published a list of some one hundred killed and disappeared persons.

In this, Croatia is not alone. Serbs also have problems with the truth. In their own eyes they are the biggest victims of both Milošević and NATO. Indeed, Serbian society suffered severe consequences – from embargoes to NATO bombing – as a result of the wars it waged against its neighbours, but the whole truth about what happened has not yet surfaced or become part of the public debate. In this respect Serbia and Croatia share a consensus about the lies of the past ten years. The reason is simple, one that goes beyond the Tudjman–Milošević ideology. Too many people were in some way involved in the war, and too many of them profited from it. It is easier, and much more comfortable, to live with lies than to confront the truth, and with that truth the possibility of individual guilt – and collective responsibility.

However, the conflict between truth and justice has serious political consequences: the governments in both Serbia and Croatia have problems with the truth and justifying to their citizens the extradition of those indicted for war crimes to the Tribunal in The Hague.

Because people find it easier to live with lies than with the truth, attempts to administer justice through the Tribunal or even through the local courts are seen as an injustice. And as long as there is so little desire in these societies to uncover the truth, the bringing to justice of war criminals will continue to be perceived as a threat to the entire community. Until then, justice simply has to come from The Hague or it will not come at all – and all because we ourselves are not capable of washing our own dirty, bloody laundry in public. We do not yet even realise the need to do it.

2

Justice Is Boring

In the Tribunal building in Churchill Square in The Hague it smells of fresh paint. A young man in white overalls is slowly painting the entrance hall, which is otherwise empty; it has big glass walls on either side. On the left is the main entrance to the offices of the court; it has a security gate, and a policeman standing guard. I want to go to courtroom number three, where the trials of Miroslav Kvočka, Dragoljub Prćac, Milojica Kos, Mladjo Radić and Zoran Žigić are taking place, all of them accused of murder and torture in the Omarska and Keraterm camps in Bosnia. There is a second security gate at the top of the marble staircase. Once I pass through it (no tape recorders or cameras allowed in the courtroom), I climb up a narrow iron staircase to the courtroom, where yet another policeman stands at the door. Courtroom number three is rather small and is divided in two by a bulletproof glass wall. The public area accommodates about a hundred people seated in uncomfortable blue plastic chairs. There are two television screens in each corner. It doesn't look like the courtrooms in the movies or in TV shows like *L.A. Law*, with their dark wood panelling. This courtroom looks more like a hospital waiting room: aseptic, with simple, functional furniture and grey wall-to-wall carpeting, lit with strong neon lights that make people look pale and sickly.

I sit in the first row because I want a clear view. But I can sit anywhere I please, because today I am the only member of the public present. I am a bit surprised – entrance is free – but it seems there is not much interest in the daily proceedings of the trials. I have been told that law students and relatives of the defendants come here from time to time, but journalists come only at the opening of a new trial and when a sentence is to be pronounced. Then it is hardly possible to squeeze yourself in. Now I am facing the three judges sitting on a kind of platform, the defendants and their lawyers to my left and the prosecution lawyers to my right. The defendants can see the public through the glass, with only a few metres separating them. The glass wall was probably put there to protect them from possible assault. But it feels to me as though I am the one being protected from the dangerous men behind it.

So I sit and watch them, the five defendants. They look so ordinary. But what did I expect to see? Horns? Pointed ears? After all, they were all ordinary policemen, except for Žigić, who was a taxi driver. Interestingly enough, he is the only one who looks threatening, maybe because he has a stronger build than the other four. Žigić is a dark man in his forties with a broad neck, dressed in a brown suit and a yellow shirt. Today his defence witness is being examined. Next to him is Prćac, an elderly man, grey-haired and thin. In his grey suit and with his small, greyish moustache he resembles a mouse. The two of them sit between two UN policemen who look as if they are thinking about last Sunday's picnic. Seated behind them, also flanked by two UN policemen, are the rest of the group: Kos and Kvočka look like village troublemakers, while the stocky Radić looks as if he could be a factory director in a small town.

Žigić is nervously shifting back and forth in his chair, as though he wants a cigarette. Surely he smokes; most Bosnian men do. He probably wants a cup of coffee too: in Bosnia they drink that strong coffee that used to be called 'Turkish coffee'. I wonder what the politically correct term is now – 'Serbian coffee'? The five men sit there, day after day, for hours on end with neither cigarettes nor coffee, listening to the translation of what the lawyers and judges are saying. Sometimes they must feel as if they are in a movie. They probably never expected to end up in a foreign court. And all that is now happening to them is so unreal that they expect the scene to fade out at any moment.

One of the judges is now examining a protected witness for the defence. A protected witness may not be seen by the public; he sits behind plastic blinds and his face is shown blurred on a TV screen. This trial has been going on for almost a year now, and if you are in a courtroom for the first time, as I am, it is not easy to follow what is happening. Not because of the topic at hand, but because of the procedure. A witness may be examined in minute detail, and it is easy to get lost if you didn't keep in mind what it is all about. Often there are procedural questions that have to be clarified, which makes it even more difficult for an observer. This witness had been a guard in the Keraterm camp, and he had been there on the night of 24 July 1992, when a massacre in one of the barracks took place, in which more than one hundred prisoners were killed. This is how the cross-examination goes:

Judge: Did you ever enter the room with prisoners?

Witness: No.

Judge: Were you near the entrance to that room? How can you tell the diameter of this barrel in front of the room number one?

Witness: The doors were open, you could see inside.

Judge: The barrel was inside or outside?

Witness: It was outside.

Judge: How do you know that the diameter was thirty centimetres?

Witness: I estimated it.

I try to follow this for some time, not sure why it is so important to establish where the barrel was, but trusting the judge that it is important. However, I find myself growing bored. I look at the accused. Žigić is trying hard to concentrate; after all, this is a witness for his defence. But one can tell by the expression on his face that he is not listening carefully. His eyes are roving around the courtroom, just as mine are. Kos is looking at the ceiling. Prćac seems to be devoting his attention to the woman whose job it is to write down every word of the trial, maybe because of the lively floral pattern of her dress. One of the defence lawyers is discreetly yawning.

The cross-examination is long, careful and exhaustive. I admire the evident concentration of the judges, while I myself feel that I may fall asleep at any moment. Now, after spending some time in this courtroom, I understand why it is empty. A trial – any trial and not just this one – is painstakingly slow and boring. But this is exactly as it should be. A trial is not a show for the audience. It does not need to be interesting or entertaining. It is a serious thing: justice is in question, human lives are at stake, and there is nothing spectacular in proving someone's guilt or innocence.

I look at my watch. Only an hour has passed, and it feels like an eternity, as if time has a different quality in this courtroom, as if it is passing more slowly in here than outside on the streets of The Hague. Perhaps it is? I try again to focus. The guard is attempting to defend Žigić, who took part in the massacre. The killing, he says, happened because prisoners tried to escape and were shot while running away. But why the blood in the room? asks the judge. Why the blood on the walls?

Blood on the walls?

Suddenly I see that picture in front of my eyes, and I realise what the judge is talking about. The death of 120 prisoners is no longer abstract, no longer mere words. Now the tedious, precise interrogation takes on a new meaning. Now I realise how much we are all poisoned by the trials depicted in television shows and Hollywood movies, with their rapid exchanges of arguments between good-looking lawyers in expensive suits. In The Hague there is no such false drama. The drama here is that everything really happened: there were real deaths, real victims and real murderers. Real blood. The drama is that there can be no escape from that reality. When at the end of that day in the court I take a long look at the defendants, they suddenly seem different to me. I see what I did not see before – not their dull faces, but a room with its walls splashed with blood.

3

A Suicide Scenario

Milan Levar, a Croatian war veteran from Gospić and a witness of war crimes, was murdered on 28 August 2000. After the trial of the 'Gospić group' a decade later, his suspected murderer, Ivica Rožić, was released because there was not enough material evidence against him.

In Gospić, a decade after the end of the war in Croatia, the war is not over, at least not for Vesna and Leon Levar. If they leave their house, they have to tell the police where they are going. Then a police patrol will accompany them on their outing. Before they are allowed to visit the grave of their husband and father, Milan Levar, the police thoroughly check the graveyard. The people from Gospić do not talk to Vesna and boys do not play football with eleven-year-old Leon. Vesna and Leon belong to the 'enemy' camp. This is very unusual in a small town of only six thousand inhabitants, especially because neither Vesna nor Leon has committed any crime. They do not even have the 'wrong' Serbian blood in their veins – there are very few Serbs living in Gospić nowadays. They are prisoners of war of a very special kind.

'At the Mass, a year after my husband's death, we were the only ones in church. And at the grave; not a single representative of the government was there,' Vesna has said. But someone visited Milan Levar's grave before her, before the funeral, because she found a flower there. A single plastic flower, but a flower nonetheless, a sign that someone cared about him. Except that that person did not have the courage to be seen at his graveside. That person was afraid because the case has not been solved yet and the murderer is still at large. Newspapers say that the police know who the murderer is, but they do not have enough evidence to arrest him.

Milan Levar was the first witness for the Tribunal to be killed in revenge. Walk down any street in Gospić and you begin to understand how much the spirit of the place contributed to the murder of Levar. It only takes about half an hour to see the entire town. Like its people, all the buildings that are left standing bear the deep scars of war: dilapidated houses with façades peeling off like burned skin, shattered windows, empty ruins and pockmarked asphalt. You cannot escape the sight of gaping walls exposing the ravaged interiors of once cosy, welcoming, solid brick homes. Their walls are blackened by fire now, fires that were ignited not only by enemy shells but also by the neighbours. There are ruins everywhere, monuments to the two months in the autumn of 1991 when thousands of shells fell on the town from the Serbian side. To wake up every day to those ruins and to remember the houses as they were before – this alone must have been enough to drive the people of Gospić to madness.

In the main street, men walk about unshaven and dressed in fatigues as if the war is still going on for them, as it is for the

Levar family. There is not much for them to do in this half-dead place nowadays, so they drink coffee and *rakija*, and talk local politics and wait for something to happen. Everyone who could left a long time ago, before the war started. People do not come back; there is nothing to come back to. Ten years ago Gospić was a pleasant, if sleepy place, where people lived quiet, comfortable lives and children could play safely in the streets. If you so much as sneezed, your neighbour would be there ready to help you. Until the day that same neighbour came to arrest you.

Now, as you enter the town, you instantly feel what dominates life here: fear. There are few people and they know everything about each other. They know what their neighbours are cooking for lunch, from which deserted or ruined house their carpet, refrigerator or television comes, and what each of them did during the war. They have good reason to be afraid of each other. It has to do with the so-called 'TV-set syndrome'. If you mention this, people will know exactly what you mean. It means that the majority of them used the war to 'help' themselves to TV sets and similar goods from deserted houses. There are others who did far worse things, of course, but if you dare to challenge them and demand justice, they will say: 'You shut up, you stole a TV set.' As if killing a man could ever be equated with stealing a TV. Of course it could not, but the comparison is enough to keep mouths shut.

Which brings us to the next thing you notice in Gospić: the silence. Indeed, there is a conspiracy of silence, something akin to the Italian *omertà*, the law of silence. Such a dangerous, threatening silence is evident in a place so small. Of course, it is not really silent; cars drive past, babies cry, people talk and loud music fills the cafés. The smothering silence only falls when you try to talk about certain subjects. For example, nobody wants to talk about what happened to Serbian civilians in October 1991, or about why Milan Levar was killed. If somebody does comment on his death at all, it is most likely a curse: 'He should have been killed sooner. He is a traitor and thank God somebody liquidated him,' said a neighbour in a matter-of-fact way only a few hours after his funeral.

You really must have been loathed to evoke such cruel, cynical words even after your death. Levar was just such a person. In a provincial town where anything different was to be abhorred, he dared to be different. He believed that justice could be done and that it was worth fighting for. Moreover, Levar believed that he could testify in court about the atrocities committed against Serbian civilians in Gospić during the war and still live a normal life among some of the very people who got their hands dirty, whether they did so by arresting Serbs, by digging their graves, by stealing furniture, or just by closing their eyes to what was really happening. But Levar could not do this. He knew their secrets, and so he became a threat to them all, critical of their way of life and of their cowardly behaviour.

He should have known better. Their hatred was palpable. He must have felt it every time he walked out of his house. He must have seen it on the faces of people who passed him every day. For his family, going shopping must have been like setting out on an expedition through hostile territory. If anyone offered sympathy, it was secretly, under cover of darkness. How would they survive besieged by curses and threats? His wife, Vesna, endured hostility every day when she was at work earning their main, albeit meagre, income. And their little boy, Leon – how many times was he called a 'Chetnik's bastard' by his schoolmates? This hatred must have got to them on occasions. They were not made of steel. It must have been even more painful for Levar because he had been born in Gospić; it was his hometown. And yet, he was convinced that he could be strong enough to fight the provincial lethargy and fear.

His biggest mistake was not his decision to tell the truth and become a witness, but his belief that he could go on living in Gospić afterwards. It was a suicide scenario. It was not possible to live among the very people he wanted to put behind bars, especially because some of those people were still in power. Instead of investigating war crimes, they covered them up. They had their own reasons for doing so and Levar knew it.

But what happened in Gospić that winter? What was it that Milan Levar witnessed? What was it that he ultimately paid for so dearly?

In the autumn of 1991 two men from Zagreb were put in charge of the defence of Gospić, although, such were the times, it is not clear by whom. Perhaps they took charge of the defence themselves. Those men were Tihomir Orešković, who became the head of the provisional civil government, and Mirko Norac, who became the head of military defence. Their names are worth remembering. They defended the town successfully against Serbian attack, but some people say that they only arrived after the battle for the defence of Gospić was over. They also understood that the aim of the war was to 'cleanse' the town of unwanted Serbs. This was a good opportunity. In the heated atmosphere of war it was enough to proclaim a person as being suspected of collaborating with the enemy. No proof was necessary. They composed a list of Serbian civilians still living in the town. In three days, from 16 to 18 October, some 120 Serbs as well as forty Croats disappeared. According to several eyewitness accounts that surfaced later – and not just that of Levar – the Serbian civilians were taken by truck to locations outside Gospić where they were executed by the military police squad under the command of Norac and buried in hidden mass graves.

For what followed no other word but pillage will suffice. The deserted houses, not only those of the murdered Serbs but also of those who had fled the town earlier, were ransacked and then burned. There were very few people who did not take part in this. It was the beginning of a reign of terror led by a small group of followers of Orešković and Norac. They did exactly as they pleased, deciding who should live and who should die while accumulating dubious wealth. Because almost no one in Gospić was innocent of the events of October 1991, everybody kept silent. And even if there were innocent people among them, they most certainly didn't dare speak. It was easy to rule in a place where everyone had to conform – that is, if he wanted to stay alive.

In this deserted town on the front line, Orešković and Norac seized power, and there was nobody to challenge them. 'In those times and in the euphoric atmosphere of war, it was easy to rule desperate people. You had so many empty houses and you could appropriate anything you wanted from them. You could do whatever you wanted with the few remaining people because both Croats and Serbs ran away, at least those who could,' Levar said later.

Milan Levar was disgusted that neither the army, the police nor anyone from the government tried to stop Orešković and Norac's reign of terror. Together with two of his colleagues from the militia, Zdenko Ropac and Zdenko Banda (both of whom later went into hiding in Germany), he contacted some important people in the Croatian government and informed them about the situation in Gospić. Levar knew what he was talking about because he himself had been forced by Orešković at gunpoint to watch while a Serb civilian was strangled with a telephone cord.

The authorities in Zagreb knew what was going on almost immediately, because the relatives of those who had disappeared had also contacted various people in the government. The government was forced to open investigations. Ante Karić, the president of the Crisis Council from Zagreb, was sent to Gospić at the beginning of November 1991 and he returned with a detailed report of the usurpation of power by the military police. People had disappeared overnight, the black market was flourishing, the deserted houses of both Croats and Serbs were in ruins. This report was sent to both President Franjo Tudjman and the Chief of the Secret Police, Josip Manolić. Again someone was dispatched to Gospić by the Office for Defence of Constitutional Order. In a report dated 20 December 1991, Rikard Pavelić described the atmosphere of terror, the mysterious disappearance of people, the discovery of new corpses every day, plundering and looting – all connected to the military police. 'For the majority of liquidated people there are witnesses that the military police took them away to Perušić and other places, where all traces of them are lost,' wrote Pavelić. 'People are taken away daily and new corpses are found.' The Chief of Police in Gospić, Ivan Dasović, had been present when a large group of Serbian civilians was liquidated. Not only did he list the people who took part in the decision-making, but he himself, as he later confessed, was at the execution site, shooting, while the commanding officer Norac was shouting, 'Shoot, shoot, what are you waiting for!'

The Croatian government and the President were informed of what was happening in Gospić, and there was enough proof of war crimes. Something needed to be done, and so Orešković was arrested. He and several other people from Gospić were brought to Zagreb and interrogated. But after the intervention of the Minister of Defence, Gojko Šušak, the investigation was suspended and Orešković was released. Šušak had an enormous influence on Tudjman and, though aware of their crimes, Tudjman agreed that it was better not to take action against Orešković and Norac.

When Levar and his companions realised that their reports to the authorities had achieved nothing but danger for themselves, they left the militia. One can only try to imagine Levar's despair. But why did he not leave Gospić then? Was it his stubborn nature that kept him there? Did he have some hidden motives? Those who knew him say that Milan Levar was an honest man, a man of principles. He did not want the new state of Croatia to be built on war crimes. But others claim that he was deranged by the war. In an interview with the independent Split weekly, *Feral Tribune*, in 1996, Levar said: 'Lika [the region of which Gospić is the capital] today is ruled by fear. In order for this fear to disappear, people have to, finally, account for their deeds. It has to be established who killed and who stole and everyone has to bear the consequences. Because in this way those who committed crimes, by keeping all power in their hands, turned us into prisoners and are treating us as slaves.'

But the problem was that the government itself was part of the conspiracy. Nobody wanted to investigate the case; it would not look good for it to become known that not just Serbs but Croats as well had committed war crimes. There was political reasoning behind hiding the truth about Gospić. This was a time when Croatia was fighting for international recognition as an independent state. The truth about the murder of Serbian civilians in Gospić could impede that recognition. It was better to cover up the whole unpleasant affair. So, the truth was buried in the name of 'higher' (political) interests. Those in power in Gospić were entrusted with keeping its secrets.

Levar came to realise that only public opinion could reverse the situation. If he could manage to muster enough popular support, the government would have to investigate Orešković and Norac again. However, when Levar told *Globus* magazine what he had witnessed, he received only threats.

Silence shrouded the whole Gospić case until 1996, when Tihomir Orešković finally tried to establish power in the Lika region by putting himself forward as a candidate for mayor of the town of Perušić. Once more Levar went to the newspapers, to the *Feral Tribune*. He got more publicity this time, and even foreign newspapers picked up on the Gospić case. But once again, the outcome was not what Levar had hoped for: the investigation was not reopened, although Orešković did withdraw his candidacy.

The public pressure Levar hoped to create did not manifest itself. Indeed, the general public seemed to be indifferent to his story. It was as if everybody, not just those in Gospić but in the whole of Croatia, was deaf and blind. Perhaps people were blinded by the 'national interest', but it is as likely that there were other, more personal, interests at stake. But this time both Levar and Zdenko Banda were threatened explicitly. Explosives were found in Levar's mother's house and in Banda's summer home in Karlobag. The message was loud and clear: stop talking, or else.

Bitter and disappointed, Levar was left with little choice but turn to the ICTY in The Hague. He had tried everything else, from offering his statement to the Croatian governmental institutions to attempting to bring the whole affair out into the open through the newspapers, all to no avail. He gave his sworn testimony to the Tribunal in 1997 and 1998. He believed that his statement in The Hague would finally force the Croatian government to begin a real investigation of the Gospić case.

People working at the Tribunal knew very well what Levar's testimony meant, and how dangerous it was. They also knew that there would no longer be a life for Levar in Gospić after he had been proclaimed a 'traitor'. So they offered to make him a protected witness, to move him and his family abroad and give them new identities. But Levar turned down the offer, believing that going public would give him enough protection. He thought that if he stayed, his presence would motivate other people to come forward as witnesses as well. He could not let them down by leaving Croatia. But he was naive; it was as if he had forgotten that he was dealing with murderers. He also had too much confidence in the Croatian legal system. Two other witnesses, his former colleagues Zdenko Banda and Zdenko Ropac, did not think twice and left for Germany.

Nevertheless, the Tribunal wanted to help Levar and demanded protection for him from the Croatian government. But was this demand passed on to the local police in Gospić? Even if it was, would the Gospić police have protected a man who was willing to give evidence about crimes committed by the military police with the collaboration of the civilian police forces? Not much had changed after the war; the same people were still there. For them, Levar was a man who knew too much and talked too much. He had been warned several times: surely he had got the message? Now he faced a serious dilemma – but it did not stop him talking.

The elections and the change of government in January 2000 must have brought him new hope, but that hope did not last long. Months passed but still there was no investigation into the Gospić case, or any other war crimes for that matter. Levar must have been terribly disappointed and may have begun to think about leaving Croatia. 'Latterly, Milan changed his mind and wanted to leave Croatia,' Vesna recalled, crying. 'I will never forgive myself for being against that.'

Seven months later, on the afternoon of 28 August 2000, Milan Levar was killed by a bomb explosion. It happened in his mother's yard. The bomb was hidden in the spare tyre of his car. His son, Leon, was present. He tried to help his father, to turn him on his back, but it was too late. 'He called me on the mobile telephone, but could not say anything. He was just screaming,' said his mother. Nobody in Gospić was surprised that Levar was killed. The town was too small for someone labelled a traitor to survive. There was no place there to hide. Being a witness in Gospić, living in a small community, was far riskier than being a witness in Zagreb, a city of a million inhabitants.

It was silence that killed Milan Levar slowly over the years, not just a bomb. The silence of neighbours; the silence of friends; the silence of the province; of public opinion as well as the cover-up of the government in Zagreb. This should have changed when Levar made all those crimes public. It was what he had hoped for: once the war crimes became public knowledge, there would be no way back to feigned ignorance and indifference.

But what do you do if you reveal a crime and nothing happens? No reaction. No pressure. Just a blanket of silence, even more suffocating than you felt it was at the time the events in Gospić took place. Levar had not expected this. He did not understand the apathy of the people in Croatia, who simply did not want to hear him and who purposely ignored facts even though they were laid out before them. He had miscalculated, and he must have asked himself why. The answer is the same as for what happened in the town of Gospić. Too many people had profited from 'ethnic cleansing' in many different, sometimes only small, ways. Moreover, even those who did not profit did not protest either. There were people who supported Levar and were willing to listen to the truth, but they were too few to be able to make a difference.

His last option was to try to stir up public opinion. Because this attempt failed so miserably, Levar is now dead. Public opinion is not an abstract concept. It is about us, what we, the citizens of Croatia, stand for. The failure of public opinion is therefore our own failure. We did not react; we have nobody but ourselves to blame. Our personal paranoia, petty theft and sealed lips all contributed to the bomb that killed Levar.

Not many people attended his funeral. Instead of turning into a mass demonstration in support of the principles for which he died, the funeral was just another episode in a long line of betrayals. Some people were too afraid to show up, but most just did not care. There were no representatives from the armed forces, no politicians, no religious dignitaries, no human rights groups and no one from the media. Their absence was more significant than their presence would have been.

After Milan Levar was murdered, things became clear. The police now had no choice but to start an investigation, not only into Levar's murder but into the Gospić case as well.

Ten years after the war crimes were committed, fear of the truth that is surfacing is still great. The Croatian state is still indecisive, the international community is indifferent and public opinion remains silent.

4

A Quiet Night in October

The trial of the 'Gospić group' was a landmark in the Croatian legal system. This is because the five men (Tihomir Orešković, Mirko Norac, Stjepan Grandić, Ivica Rožić, and Milan Čanić) were tried for killing Serbs in Gospić in the winter of 1991, not at the ICTY, but in the local court in Rijeka. Their trial lasted from June 2001 to March 2003, some 150 witnesses testified, and three of the accused were found guilty of killing fifty people. The other two were acquitted.

It was already late at night when a military truck stopped on the outskirts of Gospić, near a village called Pazarište. A military policeman lifted the tarpaulin in the back, and some twelve people stepped down on to the damp earth. As they came out of the truck, they saw the silhouettes of armed men waiting for them. They could hear the sound of the truck departing, of car doors opening and closing, of muffled voices and the clanking of arms – and then, for a minute or two, awkward silence. Somebody tried to light a cigarette nervously, but then gave up, swearing.

Suddenly, a woman's scream pierced the darkness. It was a high-pitched, short scream, followed by a shot and a man's voice: 'Shoot, shoot, what are you waiting for!' Then the small group of armed shadows started shooting. Everyone was shooting: soldiers with machine guns, civilians with pistols. It would be dangerous not to, because someone was going from man to man checking that they had fired their weapons. After a few minutes all the people from the back of the truck were dead. Armed men jumped into their cars and left hurriedly. The bodies of the dead were never found.

This happened on 16 October 1991, and it was preceded by a meeting in Gospić in the Crisis Headquarters, organised by Tihomir Orešković, the head of the civilian government – and the one who, according to witnesses, was checking the arms after the shooting. The voice in the dark giving the command to shoot was that of Mirko Norac, the military commander of Gospić. Both men were gaoled in Rijeka together with four other men from the so-called 'Gospić group'. They were indicted for ordering executions and for executing Serbian civilians; the events of the night of 16 October were only the beginning. For the next few years the life of a Serb in Gospić, or of a Croat who disagreed with the policy of the local bosses Orešković and Norac, was worth less than that of a stray dog. A report by a police investigator a year later stated that well over a hundred people disappeared into mass graves somewhere near Gospić in that single night in October.

It is hard to imagine Mirko Norac shouting the order for execution. He does not look like a soldier, much less a tough war commander. Not even a general's uniform can make him look manly and capable of such a job. A plump, plain young man with a shy smile and a double chin, he looks more soft than dangerous. People who know him say that his most important characteristic is loyalty, and this could be the reason he rose so quickly in the hierarchy of the Croatian Army, eventually reaching the rank of general.

Norac actually looks like what he really is – a waiter. It is much easier to imagine him in a café in Sinj, serving coffee and beer to the locals and chatting with them about Sunday's football matches. Not that Norac spent much time working as a waiter; he was not at all keen to work as long as his father was sending enough money home from Germany where he worked on building sites. Norac was not mad about school either. He only just completed two years at the school from which he qualified as a waiter, later followed by several courses at a military college. He was considered neither particularly bright nor especially diligent. In his small village of Otok, near Sinj, it was common for people to become priests or nuns; Otok is famous for having provided thirty-five men for the priesthood and 170 women who took vows as nuns. Norac's uncle and a nephew are priests, too, and he himself was a ministrant in the church. There is no mystery here; the people of Otok are no more Catholic than others in Croatia, but in this part of Croatia there is extreme poverty. People have very few options. One is to become a priest, the other a soldier or a policeman.

Norac might have become a priest, but he became a soldier instead. Providence helped him in this. At twenty-three, jobless, not knowing what to do with himself, in August 1991 he joined the first group of volunteer soldiers and ended up in a special unit near Zagreb.

That autumn, he and three friends went to Gospić with the intention of organising the defence of the town against Serbian attack. It is not clear whether they were posted there by the Minister of Defence, Gojko Šušak, or if they ended up in

Gospić through their own initiative and connections. Information about this is contradictory. It was a chaotic period, and every new trial at the Tribunal proves the existence of parallel command, the official one (the government) and the unofficial one (the HDZ, or Croatian Democratic Union, the party line of command). While the official history says that Norac organised the defence under his own command and the Croatian Army stabilised the front line, there are witnesses who say that Norac appeared in Gospić to take over power after the town had already been defended by its citizens.

Before the war, Gospić had a mixed population. About 30 per cent were Serbs, and most of them left Gospić at the beginning of the war. However, the task of Norac and Tihomir Orešković, the head of the civil government in the town, who came with Norac from Zagreb, was not only to defend the town. It was also to 'ethnically cleanse' Gospić; that is, to get rid of the Serbs completely. Was it an order from the very top, by the Minister of Defence, Gojko Šušak, or even by President Franjo Tudjman? Perhaps there was no need to give such an order at all. Tudjman's political messages were clear enough, and both Norac and Orešković understood that defence was one thing, while the long-term goal of the war in Croatia was quite another. Besides, they were both members of a small radical right-wing emigrant party, the Croatian Statehood Party (HDP).

After Gospić, Norac took part in the 'Medak pocket' action in 1993 and in the 'Storm' action in 1995 in Krajina against the Serbian Rebel Army. He became the commander of the Knin Corps and the youngest general in the Croatian Army. The war was over. He continued to live peacefully in Zagreb, enjoying the privileges attached to his high rank and his status as war veteran and hero. He had a nice apartment, a good car and plenty of money. Not bad for a former waiter from Otok.

The years passed until one day in August 2000 a bomb exploded in a yard in Gospić. That bomb killed Milan Levar, the man who claimed that executions in Gospić were not incidental but part of the 'ethnic cleansing' campaign – which was actually the very war strategy of Tudjman's government.

Less than a month later, the arrest of five suspects was ordered, and the investigation began in the court in Rijeka. Tihomir Orešković was among those arrested.

But then something unexpected happened. The beginning of the investigation of war crimes in Rijeka brought with it a series of protests. The government was aware that public opinion was against extraditing war criminals to the Tribunal in The Hague, but now it even began to turn against a trial in Croatia itself.

The protests were staged by the organisations of war veterans. Former soldiers perceived both extradition to The Hague and the arrest of the 'Gospić group' as a great injustice. After being praised for defending Croatia against the Serbian aggressor, suddenly they were under suspicion of committing war crimes. But nobody had told them that what they had done – for example, killing Serbian civilians – was wrong. On the contrary, these same men had been awarded medals and apartments, pensions and other privileges.

Ten years later the political line in Zagreb had be redrawn, and what had earlier been implicitly approved now had to be investigated. Some war veterans feared that such investigations might involve them as well. The government was well aware that in many cases war heroes were indeed war criminals. But how to persuade people of this when they had been led to believe that such accusations were unjust and impossible?

The veterans were clamorous; they protested against the accusations of war crimes levelled at war heroes. They called it 'shameful criminalisation of the war for the Homeland'.

They also suggested that the government should hold a referendum on the question of extradition. Moreover, they openly called for the overthrow of the socialist-dominated coalition government. The leaders of the street demonstrations claimed that judging a war hero was humiliating, that bringing one to trial put the whole idea of the war itself on trial, along with the entire Croat nation. They called it a betrayal of national interests and demanded amnesty for all suspected war criminals.

After the war, the veterans' organisations grew into a very powerful political instrument controlled by the right-wing Tudjman's HDZ party. Just how powerful an instrument became clear only when they organised demonstrations in Split on 11 March 2001. On that day tens of thousands of people attended a rally in support of General Mirko Norac. Some days before this meeting, an order to arrest Norac had been issued. He was supposed to join Tihomir Orešković in prison in Rijeka. But instead of surrendering to the police, Norac went into hiding.

Why was there such an uproar about Norac? Why are people in Croatia so upset about trials of the war veterans at home – and even more upset about the Tribunal in The Hague? Why do Croatians find it so difficult to put on trial, or deliver to the Tribunal, suspected war criminals? Until 2002 Croatia had not extradited a single Croat from Croatia proper: Dario Kordić, Tihomir Blaškić, the brothers Kupreškić, Mladen Naletilić Tuta and Vinko Martinović are all Croats from Bosnia. If they later acquired Croatian citizenship, as they may have done, they fall into a different category. Tudjman delivered these men to the Tribunal in The Hague without much resistance from the veterans.

The new, post-Tudjman government is no more eager to investigate war crimes than its predecessor, nor is it any more enthusiastic about extraditing Croatian war criminals to the Tribunal in The Hague. For a decade Croatian citizens had been exposed to Franjo Tudjman's propaganda machine, which claimed that Croatian soldiers defending their country could not be committing war crimes. This was the official doctrine and everyone accepted it. If there was any investigation at all, the defendants were quickly released either because there was not enough evidence against them or because mistakes were made in the course of the investigation (as in the case of the murder of the Serbian Zec family with the twelve-year-old daughter). When the new government handed over Rahim Ademi, a Croatian citizen of Albanian nationality, there was no reaction from the veterans. But when, later on, The Hague asked for another Croatian, General Ante Gotovina, to be extradited to the Tribunal, veterans staged protests once again. Gotovina went into hiding, where he remains. After years of Tudjman's propaganda, it is still difficult and dangerous to admit the truth – that Croatian soldiers could and did commit war crimes.

Norac, the first general of the Croatian Army accused of war crimes, was considered a hero of the defence of Gospić. When he disappeared, the entire country went into a state of fervour. People were polarised: some thought he had done the right thing because it was a disgrace to extradite 'our boys' to the Tribunal in The Hague. Others took the more 'legalistic' angle – that is, even if they were against delivering their fellow Croatians to the Tribunal, they were aware that Croatia had to fulfil its international obligations. This uproar lasted for about two weeks, during which time the entire country was in thrall to the Norac case. The socialist government (in fact a coalition of six parties dominated by the socialists) was also polarised by how to deal with the problem. In the end, Prime Minister Ivica Račan had to persuade Norac to surrender to the police.

Before Norac's surrender the entire government had almost collapsed. Right-wing parties, especially the HDZ, were hoping for exactly this, whereupon new elections would take place and would give them, so they believed, a chance to seize power again. Although the Prime Minister managed to save his government, the fact that the veterans' demonstrations could produce a crisis of such magnitude made him aware of the kind of power he was dealing with, not least because the veterans' political protests also turned into something else: the veterans were joined by the poor and unemployed, unhappy that the government was not fulfilling its promises, thus turning the rally into a potentially explosive social uprising.

As a result of the uproar over the Norac case, enormous pressure was exerted on the government and on the judges. In addition to the demonstrations, the war veterans threatened to block roads and stop traffic, an action that would have destroyed the tourist season. Certain police and military units openly refused to carry out orders. Then many politicians began to raise their voices against the arrest of the suspected war criminals, and three right-wing parties demanded that parliament rule that Norac could not be arrested. This would mean overriding the court's decision – an example of direct pressure on the legal system. The veterans began to stage their demonstrations in front of the court building in Rijeka, waving banners bearing threatening slogans. The judges also received death threats, which, after the death of Milan Levar, had to be taken seriously.

But political pressure has not been the only difficulty facing the court in Rijeka. The biggest problem has been with witnesses, who can be divided into roughly two groups: executioners – those who took part in executions; and victims – those who were imprisoned and saved by chance or who witnessed the disappearance of their loved ones.

Men who participated in the meeting of the evening of 16 October 1991 and the executions following it have tried to minimise their own role or show that they were forced by the others to shoot. Their memory served them well, however, when they were asked to describe details of the executions. They remembered the time of the day, which car they used, how the people in the truck behaved, and so on. But they experienced a curious loss of memory when it came to naming those who organised the meeting, ordered executions and shot civilians.

Some of the five accused have claimed that they don't remember taking part in such a meeting, or any executions, no matter that other participants confirmed that they were there. Some, both accused and witnesses, have changed their statements. In his first statement, one of the witnesses, Siniša Glušac, said that he was ordered by Mirko Norac to execute Serbian civilians. Two days later, Glušac said he remembered nothing and that his earlier statement had been made under the influence of medication. One witness, Fatima Skula, a secretary to Tihomir Orešković, was badly beaten up after she gave an interview to *Globus* in which she claimed that she had seen Serbian civilians being killed in the building of the Crisis Headquarters. Perhaps the next time she is asked to remember something she will be suffering from amnesia. To make the trial even more difficult and more absurd, the defence lawyers have declared that, since there are no corpses, no crime could have been committed!

The pressure on the prosecution witnesses in Rijeka and their fear of revenge are so great that many witnesses prefer to keep their mouths shut or to lie, even at the risk of being punished for committing perjury or for contempt of court. As they see it, any punishment handed out by the court would be nothing compared to the threats they receive from other sources.

But there are some witnesses who speak out, those who have lost a husband, a brother, a father or a mother. They have been told that if they testify, they 'will end up the same way as members of their family in 1991', as one witness said, but this has not stopped them; they've already lost too much. They have testified not only about death squads, men with masked faces who collected people in the middle of the night, but also about the burning and looting of their houses by Croatian soldiers. Branka Krajnović, who lost both her parents, testified not only that they were taken away and never seen again, but also about her neighbours, the husbands of her friends, who placed explosives in Serbian houses. This kind of testimony is even more painful, because only a few men took part in executing civilians, while many more were involved in destroying and stealing their property.

There is a big difference between being a witness in a court in Rijeka, with war veterans demonstrating outside the building and relatives and friends of the accused sitting in the courtroom, and being a witness at the Tribunal in The Hague. In Rijeka, witnesses are much more vulnerable to harassment and threats. It is this atmosphere of fear and hostility that causes collective amnesia. How can witnesses speak out when not only are judges being threatened but the public itself is not prepared to hear the truth?

Just how strong the anti-Tribunal feelings continue to be can be judged by the fact that Mirko Norac, together with two other generals wanted by The Hague Tribunal, was proclaimed an honorary citizen of the Split and Dalmatian region in April 2002 – that is, after the investigation of the 'Gospić group' had been completed and the trial had begun.

According to the ICTY, there are between fifteen and twenty-five thousand people who should be tried for war crimes committed in Croatia and Bosnia. The Hague will take over some two hundred suspects from the highest echelons, and the rest are to be tried in local courts. The trial of the 'Gospić group' is supposed to prove that we are capable of doing it ourselves. It is the first experiment of its kind in Croatia. It is supposed to demonstrate that it is indeed possible for a country to judge its own war criminals instead of depending upon The Hague to do so, and that the Croatian legal system, as well as public opinion, is up to the task.

It is easy to agree with those who say that to allow the extradition of Croatian war criminals to the Tribunal makes us look like a second-rate country, not a state ruled by law; that it makes us look bad, as if we cannot be a democracy and that our legal system is incapable of prosecuting its own citizens. It is true that it is humiliating, and that trying them at home should force our country to confront itself with some deeply unpleasant truths about the war – and, finally, to close this chapter of history.

But what is happening in Croatia during the trials in Rijeka and Split is just the opposite. It is as if we are all deliberately closing our eyes. Thanks to the courageous female judge, Ika Šarić, who, on 23 March 2003, sentenced Tihomir Orešković to fifteen years in prison, Mirko Norac to twelve years and Stjepan Grandić to ten (while Ivica Rožić and Milan Čanić were acquitted) there is hope that Croats will be able to face their bloody past. This trial was important for another reason as well. It was the first time that the national doctrine claiming that Croats could not, in a defensive war, commit war crimes was finally questioned.

5

Boys Just Had Fun

Dragoljub Kunarac, Radomir Kovač and Zoran Vuković – Bosnian Serbs from the town of Foča in Republika Srpska – were the first men in European legal history to be sentenced for torture, slavery, outrages upon human dignity and the mass rape of Bosnian Muslim women as crimes against humanity. On 22 February 2002, at the International Tribunal for the former Yugoslavia (ICTY) in The Hague, they were sentenced to twenty-eight, twenty and twelve years in prison respectively. Six months later, on appeal, their sentences were confirmed.

I don't remember her face, or even if I saw it at all. It was probably blurred. Many women who testified in the Foča case were protected from the public by a screen, and their faces, and sometimes their voices, were blurred and distorted. But I do remember her voice – or the absence of it.

This woman came to the Tribunal as a witness in the case of Dragoljub Kunarac, Radomir Kovač and Zoran Vuković –

the so-called 'Foča case' – but when her turn came she could not speak. She sat facing Kovač, the man who had kept her daughter imprisoned, the man who raped her and finally sold her to a Montenegrin soldier for some two hundred German marks. She had last seen her child boarding a bus taking people away from Foča. Ten years passed, the war ended but her daughter never came back. Now the woman looked at Kovač, but no words came. As if someone's hand was squeezing her throat. She tried – you could see that she tried very hard to speak – but all she could utter was a tiny sound.

In the courtroom, the prosecutor showed her a photograph of her daughter (called A. B. in the court) and asked how old she had been when the picture was taken. Instead of answering the woman began to cry. But it was not really crying. It sounded as if there was a microphone inside her belly and you could hear the sobs from within tearing her apart. It lasted for no more than half a minute, that deep, whining sound, that strange howl like that of an animal so wounded that there was no other sound it could make.

The girl A. B. was twelve years old when she was taken by Kovač, a man in his forties. I remember when my own daughter was twelve. She had barely got her period, wore glasses and sneakers, and was not allowed to go to the cinema on her own. She was only a child, just as at twelve A. B. was a child. Kovač was not just a rapist but also a child molester. Not that the distinction mattered much to the girl's mother. What probably mattered to her was to see justice done, to see him punished – although there is no punishment severe enough for what he did, and no punishment would bring her daughter back. Perhaps it was also important to her to tell her story after so many years, to get it out – although in the end all she could manage was that odd sound.

To listen to that utterance was unbearable. I can't bear to hear a dog howling, let alone a human being. There is no greater pain in this world than to lose a child. And she had to sit in front of Kovač and talk about it. And the pain overwhelmed her.

Listening to her cry, Kovač was clearly not impressed. He did not move or change the expression on his face. Maybe he did not hear that sound; he looked as though what was going on in the courtroom did not concern him very much. And the contrast between the weeping mother and the indifferent Kovač summed up this trial: from the point of view of the defendants it was a complete misunderstanding.

Kovač certainly showed no sign of guilt.

He was a tall, slender man with a long face and short hair. He was even quite good looking, or at least better looking than his two pals from Foča. Except for that expression on his face. That small, cynical smile almost permanently fixed, which made him look cocky, as if, for some reason known only to himself, he felt superior to the court. I can't help thinking he should have been held in contempt of court for that smile. Dressed in a dark grey suit, which in his former life he had probably worn only for weddings and funerals, he leant back in his chair, as though relaxing. Kovač really looked like somebody you could trust to give your daughter a lift to hospital. And he might have done so, before the war. But this was after the war. You couldn't trust him. He would have raped her, even a child of twelve. Then he would have enslaved her, together with other girls of fifteen to twenty. Eventually he would have sold her to a Montenegrin soldier and she would never have been seen again.

One of the other rapists from Foča, Dragoljub Kunarac, was a rather short man in his forties with two strong, vertical lines marking his deeply sunken cheeks. His face was hard, as if carved out of wood. He looked dried up, the type of skinny but tough man you often find in mountain villages. His dark, curly hair was receding on top and looked untidy, as if he didn't wash it very often. He had big dark eyes. Nothing about him was pleasant, and it was not difficult to imagine him in camouflage uniform with a gun in his hand. Unlike Kovač, he leant forward and watched the judges with a frown, a tense expression on his face.

When you heard what the third man, Zoran Vuković, did – raped young girls, including one no older than fifteen – you would have liked to have been able to say that he looked dangerous. But he looked unthreatening, small and weak, especially next to Kovač. He had fair hair and greyish skin and looked pasty. He had no chin, and this seemed to be his main feature. At the beginning of the trial he had a short beard, probably to compensate for his lack of a chin. On that day, 22 February 2001, the day of the sentencing, he was clean-shaven and his chin seemed to disappear into his chubby neck. His face revealed no emotion. Perhaps he had none. According to the prosecution he seemed to be less cruel than the others, or perhaps they simply had less proof of his deeds, although one witness described how Vuković had told her that he had had to kill her uncle. He had had to, he insisted to her, as if asking for her understanding. Vuković, though the oldest of the three men, seemed to prefer to be led by others. But he was no less cruel or sleazy. After raping a fifteen-year-old girl, he had told her that he could have been more brutal with her but had not been, because he had a daughter the same age.

If you had met any of these three men before the war, you would probably not have thought of them as particularly violent. They were not very different from other men – just three guys who liked to hang out in local bars. Then the war came, and now it is over. Next thing you know, they are in prison. You read in the newspapers about what they did, and you wonder if it is really possible. Can ordinary men behave like that? Your neighbours, perhaps? Your relatives? No, it cannot be. They look so normal. You look for some obvious sign of perversity, some sign that will help you recognise them as criminals.

'They were low-life people who would go around and beg for cigarettes,' said one witness about the three men from Foča. 'But when the war broke out, as soon as they managed to put their hands on some rifles, they began to feel big and strong. They were only brave with us women and children.' Perhaps this witness is right: perhaps low-life men can easily turn into war criminals. Perhaps the presiding judge, Florence Mumba, was also right when she said, 'What the sum of evidence manifestly demonstrates is the effect a criminal personality will have in times of war on helpless members of the civilian population.'

But if she is right, there must have been many such 'criminal personalities' around to be able to rape tens of thousands of women and to kill more than two hundred thousand people during the war. There would have had to have been thousands of men committing such acts. Were the majority of them 'criminal personalities'? This is hard to believe. More likely, the war itself turned ordinary men – a driver, a waiter and a salesman, as were the three accused – into criminals because of opportunism, fear and, not least, conviction. Hundreds of thousands had to have been convinced that they were right in what they were doing. Otherwise such vast numbers of rapes and murders simply cannot be explained – and this is even more frightening.

The trial must have seemed surreal to the three accused men: the courtroom with the glass wall between the court and the public; the lawyers dressed in long black robes; the judges also in black robes, but with purple-red collars; the aseptic, formal atmosphere; the foreign languages all the participants spoke.

From their small town in the mountains they could not have imagined that the world would be interested in what they had done, that it would create a special court and accuse them of rape as a crime against humanity, and that a woman – a black woman! they'd hardly seen one before except on television – would preside over the court. How strange and inexplicable it must have been to sit in a prison in some foreign country far in the north, a place they had never even considered visiting, and to be judged by foreigners. Day in and day out they sat there, Kovač, Kunarac and Vuković, listening to the women speaking up against them. Not one of the men showed any remorse.

The mother of the young girl A. B. was one of some thirty women who took the stand as a witness against the rapists from Foča. They were nameless women, referred to only as FWS-87, FWS-191, FWS-50, or by their initials. A court usher would roll down a plastic yellow curtain over a part of the glass wall separating the public from the court. Obscured to the public, their voices sounding almost mechanical, almost metallic, they were nonetheless face to face with the defendants.

The three rapists from Foča probably never imagined that their victims would confront them in a courtroom. They knew that women didn't speak about their 'shame', especially not Muslim women. This time they were wrong. Raped Bosnian women decided not only to speak up, but also to do so in front of the International Criminal Tribunal. Often they cried, but they managed to describe precisely how they were taken first to a motel, Buk Bijela, then to the Foča high school and the Partizan hall, and from there to private apartments where they were turned into slaves and sexually abused for months on end.

Sometimes they were forced to 'entertain' Kovač and his pals before being raped by them. Witness FWS-87 recalled several incidents when she and other girls had to strip and dance naked on a table at gunpoint. At other times they were raped to the sweet sound of classical music. 'It was so humiliating because I felt as if I was owned by him,' FWS-87 said. One girl said that she was forced with a knife at her throat to walk naked through the streets of Foča and down to the river. Some girls were beaten, others were lent, rented out or sold to other soldiers; others simply disappeared. One said that she was raped by twenty soldiers on the first day, the same day her mother was killed. And for certain sexual offences witnesses didn't even have words to describe them to the court.

There are many men just like the trio from Foča, a small town in the Bosnian mountains, who did the same things they did. It is likely that many of them will never be brought to justice. The Bosnian government estimates that some sixty thousand women were raped. The rape of Bosnian women was an instrument of terror used against the Muslim population, part of the attempt to 'ethnically cleanse' Bosnia, and the court recognised it as such during the trial. Very few Muslims now live in Foča, renamed Srbinje, which is today a part of Republika Srpska.

The rule of the International Tribunal in The Hague is that every prisoner, when brought before the judges for the first time, has to plead either guilty or not guilty. All the war criminals brought to the court have, with only a few exceptions, pleaded not guilty. Kunarac was one of them, first pleading guilty, but then changing his mind.

In the case of these three rapists, you really wonder what they mean when they say that they are not guilty. Those who killed or ordered killings can say that they had to do so in order not to be killed themselves, and we can perhaps see this as an explanation of their deeds, of why they would plead not guilty, although it is not a justification. But the soldiers were not ordered to rape, just generally encouraged to do so, because it is an efficient way of frightening and humiliating people, which was certainly the aim of Republika Srpska armed forces in Bosnia. When they say they are not guilty, do the defendants think that the prosecution won't be able to prove their guilt, or are they convinced that there is nothing to feel guilty about? After all, even if they were a bit rough with the girls, they did not kill them, and they did not order them to be killed, like some others tried in that very same courtroom did. For example, compared to the crimes of someone like Goran Jelisić, who actually murdered people with his own hands, the crimes committed by the trio from Foča do not even look like crimes, at least not in their eyes. In their part of the world men often treat their own wives as nothing more than cattle. The man is the boss, the woman should shut up and obey him, and it is not unusual for a man beat up his wife in order to remind her of that. Rape? What is rape anyway? To take a woman when you want and wherever you want? It is a man's right, no question, as far as his wife is concerned. For raping other women, a man could get up to fifteen years imprisonment, but most of those sentenced at home get away with just one or two years. Compared to murder, rape is no big deal. With these girls the three of them just wanted to have a little fun. Sometimes they were drunk and did not even know what they were doing. Sometimes they tested their power over the girls. But they did not mean to harm them.

When the witness FWS-50 was asked how she felt after having been gang-raped, she answered, 'I felt dead.' But she was not dead, and if you asked Kunarac, Kovač and Vuković they would probably say she ought to be grateful to them for that. They had power; they could have killed the girls. Or others could have killed them. After all, these girls were their prisoners. Kovač even claimed that by keeping the girls in his apartment, he saved their lives. Compared to the mass executions going on around them every day, rape was a harmless little game. These girls were lucky to stay alive, they thought.

Lucky? I met women who had been raped. I talked to them. I especially remember one woman, a mother of two, from Kozarac. She had recently come from the Omarska camp. When I greeted her she did not look me in the eye. She had lost that habit in the camp. In her quick glances I recognised fear. She held her head bent slightly forward, as if expecting a blow at any moment. She knew some of her rapists in the camp by name – they were from a neighbouring village – but this did not help her. She described the feeling of humiliation, of absolute helplessness, of a kind of absence from her own body; she told of her desire to disappear, to die instantly. The rape left her feeling dirty, she said, as though she had been wrapped up in a layer of filth, almost like a blanket. She scrubbed herself meticulously over and over, but the feeling did not go away for a long time. She imposed a quarantine on herself: she did not allow her children to touch her, afraid that she would besmirch them as well. She was alive, yes, but she did not consider herself lucky.

The presiding judge, Florence Mumba, was a black woman from Zambia with a beautiful, serene face and traditionally plaited hair. When the three rapists from Foča heard that she had been appointed to their case, they must have been convinced of their bad luck. What could a rapist expect from a female judge? Of course she would be hard on them, of course she would go for the maximum sentence. Besides, she was not even from Europe, so what could she know about the war? She might think that the three of them saw an opportunity only to gratify themselves; she could not understand that Serbs and Muslims were enemies, and that therefore to dishonour Muslim women was . . . well, somehow legitimate. Everybody was doing it. In their own country, Republika Srpska, they were treated like heroes. Who would arrest them? Who would volunteer to be a witness against them? Their victims came as witnesses to The Hague, yes, but they would not dare to do the same in Foča or Sarajevo, or anywhere else in Bosnia for that matter. They would be afraid that their own people would recognise them.

If it were not for The Hague, Kunarac, Kovač and Vuković would still be sitting in a café in Foča's main street, smoking, drinking brandy and telling stories about the war. They would be given the respect that war veterans get there. And if by accident one of the women they raped happened to pass by, they would point at her – and laugh.

On 22 February 2001, Judge Florence Mumba asked the three defendants to stand up. She was ready to deliver the sentences, but first she would explain to each of them why they were being sentenced and make sure that each of them really understood. Addressing the courtroom, she said, 'The three accused are not ordinary soldiers, whose morals were merely loosened by the hardships of war. These are men with no known criminal past. However, they thrived in the dark atmosphere of the dehumanisation of those believed to be enemies, when one would not even ask, in the words of Eleanor Roosevelt, "Where, after all, do universal human rights begin? In small places, close to home." Political leaders and war generals are powerless if the ordinary people refuse to carry out criminal activities in the course of war. Lawless opportunists should expect no mercy, no matter how low their position in the chain of command may be.'

Dragoljub Kunarac was first to be sentenced. He stood and listened carefully to Judge Mumba's words. It was not a long speech, but too long for someone waiting for a sentence. Then she finally turned to him. After listing his crimes, she concluded, 'By the totality of these acts you have shown the most glaring disrespect for the women's dignity and their fundamental human right to sexual self-determination, on a scale that far surpasses even what one might call, for lack of a better expression, the "average seriousness of rapes during wartime". You abused and ravaged Muslim women because of their ethnicity, and from among their number, you picked whomsoever you fancied on a given occasion . . . You not only mistreated women and girls yourself, but you also organised their transfer to other places, where, as you were fully aware, they would be raped and abused by other soldiers. This behaviour calls for a severe penalty commensurate with the gravity of your crimes. The Trial Chamber therefore sentences you, Dragoljub Kunarac, to a single sentence of twenty-eight years imprisonment. The sentence shall run from today. The time you have spent in custody shall be credited towards the sentence. You may sit down.'

There was a brief moment, a few seconds, before Judge Mumba's words were translated into Kunarac's language, when hope was still visible on his face. Then he understood and bent his head as if something had hit him. He probably expected a lighter punishment because he had turned himself in, cooperated with the prosecution and even said that he was sorry for the one rape that he admitted to. Now, suddenly, he must have realised that he would be almost seventy when he got out of prison, and I could tell that he didn't quite believe that he had been given such a sentence.

Radomir Kovač's expression didn't change a bit when his turn came. While Judge Mumba enumerated his crimes, he listened with the same idiotic little smile, looking as if he had nothing to do with it, as if he was in the courtroom by sheer accident. But the judge, if she noticed it at all, was not bothered by it and in her calm voice told him, 'Particularly appalling and deplorable is your treatment of the twelve-year-old A. B., a helpless little child for whom you showed absolutely no compassion whatsoever, but whom you abused sexually in the same way as the other girls. You finally sold her like an object, in the knowledge that this would almost certainly mean further sexual assaults by other men . . . The treatment of her is the most striking example of your morally depraved and corrupt character . . . You relish the absolute power you exerted over their lives, which you made abundantly clear by making them dance naked on a table while you watched.' When Kovač heard that he was sentenced to twenty years in prison, he did not even blink.

The third accused, Zoran Vuković, must by now have been aware that his sentence wouldn't be light either. He, too, was charged with torture and rape, but for his crimes he got twelve years because, as it was explained, only one of the incidents underlying those charges had been proven. 'The Trial Chamber regards it as a serious matter that you showed a total lack of remorse and moral stature by talking about your own daughter after having raped Witness FWS-50, who was in addition only fifteen years old at the time, and mocked her in her grief by saying that you could have treated her much worse still,' Judge Mumba said, taking a long look at all three men, as if she wanted to be certain that they understood her, and understood her well.

Nevertheless, for the three defendants this trial seemed to be a misunderstanding. In spite of the long sessions, the many witnesses and Judge Mumba's excellent speech, none of them fully grasped why he was being punished. The words they had just heard from the judge were too abstract for them, empty words from someone who did not comprehend their situation, or so they believed. The girls were alive, were they not? Otherwise how could they come to The Hague and be witnesses against the three of them? Even the girl A. B. could still be alive somewhere in Montenegro.

They heard their sentences and were visibly devastated by the 'injustice' done to them. Twenty-eight years, twenty years, twelve years for rape, while real murderers were getting much less in the same court? Was that justice? There were many other men in Bosnia doing even worse things to women. Why them? Why were only the three of them being so severely punished? Looking at these three men, I could tell that they would serve their sentences regretting only that they had been stupid enough to get caught or been tricked into surrendering.

6

He Would Never Hurt a Fly

Goran Jelisić, a Bosnian Serb born in 1968 in Bijeljina, was sentenced to forty years in prison for executing thirteen prisoners in May 1992 in a Brčko police station and at the Luka camp near Brčko. But it seems that he actually executed many more than a hundred. Most of the prisoners were Muslims.

Goran Jelisić looks like a man you can trust.

This young man of thirty, with his clear, serene face, lively eyes and big, reassuring grin, would make you feel safe sitting next to him in a train compartment at night. A man with such a face usually helps elderly women to cross a street, he will stand up in a tram to let an invalid sit down or he will let you go ahead of him in a supermarket queue. He will return a lost wallet to its owner. Jelisić looks like your best friend, your trusted neighbour, your ideal son-in-law. If he had been a salesman, he would surely have great success with that innocent face of his.

But he is not innocent.

We tend to believe that good-looking people are good, just as we sometimes consider ugly people to be mean. It doesn't have much to do with reality, of course. But I had never seen such a compellingly naive, boyish face on a killer, and I must say that I was overcome with surprise.

Goran Jelisić was born in 1968, which makes him the same age as my daughter. They belong to the same generation. They could have gone to the same school. They could have been friends. I could imagine him sitting in my kitchen on a winter's afternoon with a cup of tea, bent over a textbook with my daughter explaining to him their history homework (he was not a good pupil and left high school after the first year). I could imagine the two of them going to a cinema or a disco together. I would not have objected to that: he has such a sweet face. I have seen many young men like him pass through my kitchen, confused, not interested in school, but otherwise well-behaved and pleasant. Because Jelisić lived in Bijeljina, he probably did not travel abroad very much or speak any foreign languages, seldom listened to the latest music. But nevertheless, he was of the same generation as my daughter and her friends.

Their generation grew up healthy. There was no formula milk and no baby food yet, so we mothers had to cook soup for them and prepare spinach and carrots and fruit juices. There were no Pampers then either, and cotton nappies are very unpleasant when they are soaking wet, so they learned quickly to ask for the potty. As children they played outside, in the yards, in parks, on pavements in front of houses. There was no danger, at least none that we were aware of at that time.

As they got older, they were convinced that they were no different from their peers in the West, because they listened to

U2 and Madonna, watched American movies and TV shows, read Tolkien and wore jeans, just as if it were perfectly normal in Yugoslavia. For my generation, living in a communist country, jeans were a product of the 'Western bourgeois society' and a sign of decadence; my father would never have allowed me to wear them. But communism meant little to my daughter's generation, and Tito even less. They were young children when he died in 1980 and hardly remembered him at all. They had not been marked by the cult of Tito as much as we were. My generation had a strong collective identity. We had grown up solemnly celebrating Tito's birthday – the 'Day of Youth' – on 25 May every year at school, celebrating what we believed he meant for Yugoslavia. We were educated as his children, his pioneers.

In a way, the children of the late sixties are the first normal generation. Their grandparents fought in the Second World War. Their parents grew up in poverty. They grew up during a time of security and abundance. I had to eat all the food on my plate, but my daughter did not. War for them was something they learned about in history lessons or saw in movies. It had happened more than twenty years before they were even born, and it was not quite real. For my generation, the war was much closer. Even if our parents did not speak about it, we knew they still lived with the traumas of war. I hated the Germans for what they had done to my father, but my daughter's generation was indifferent to them.

Their generation was apolitical, too. They learned that politics was for grown-ups. The older generation kept them out of politics on purpose – as we had been as well. And it looked as though communism would never die, so why bother getting involved? But they were not brought up as a rebellious generation. This is because we, their parents, were true believers. We believed what we were told, that 'socialism with a human face' was possible, and we did not think that a democratic alternative had to be created. When communism collapsed, we found ourselves without political leaders equipped with democratic ideas. But this vacuum was soon filled with nationalist leaders, or with communists already in power, like Slobodan Milošević, who turned nationalist because it was an easy way to stay in power.

Our children believed that we, their parents, would sort out the political mess. But we did not. When the war broke out, they did not understand that they, born in the late sixties or early seventies, were expected to fight it. But who else could? This was a paradox: this generation, in a way, had to fight the war of their grandparents. The price was high: many of them were killed, wounded or turned into invalids, while many others fled the country.

Goran Jelisić loved fishing.

He liked dancing with girls and drinking beer with his pals, but most of all he liked fishing. He could hang out by the river day after day. He had several favourite spots that only he knew about, and when he wanted to fish alone he would go there. Not that he did not like company; on the contrary, he enjoyed competitions and being part of a fishing team. But sometimes he preferred to be alone. His friends from the fishing club would only talk about politics and drink beer, would pay no attention to their fishing rods. For Goran fishing was a time out from his daily life. This was the best thing about fishing: you could forget about the world, even forget about yourself, and concentrate just on the surface of the water and the thin nylon thread. It was almost as if you didn't exist, as if you were a tree or a leaf or grass. Goran enjoyed the feeling when nothing really matters, when who you are is not important, because the river doesn't care about it and neither do the fish.

There was not much to forget, though, at least not before the war. He was aware that his life was just plain and straightforward and that he was not particularly good at anything, except perhaps fishing.

Goran was a good fisherman, and he was not mean. He often gave fish away to friends or neighbours, to a man in whose house he later stayed after he left the Luka camp. He fished for the pleasure of it, but no one could say that Goran was fishing only for himself. He knew places with more fish in them than others, so choosing a place was very important; the rest, of course, was luck.

It was always peaceful by the river. There was something about being alone with nature, a feeling as if you were the only man alive. Nobody telling you what to do. You could be your own master. Once Jelisić fell asleep in the grass. When he woke up, he did not know where he was. He did not feel his own body. All he saw was a deep blue sky. He got scared. For a split second it occurred to him that he might be dead. Perhaps this is how one feels when one is dead, a sort of a total absence, he thought. Then he came back, knew that he was alive, glad that he was catching fish. Once somebody – a woman, of course – asked him if he felt sorry for the fish. Sorry? What an amazing thought; it never occurred to him that he could feel anything for the fish. It is the law of nature that rules, and fish are lower beings, he told her. If not, they would be the ones catching us.

You have to be very patient to spend all day fishing. Fishing is not a sport for nervous, aggressive people. In his love of fishing, Jelisić reminds me of my son-in-law, who also loves fishing more than football or going to the cinema. He carefully prepares for fishing, selecting rods, hooks, bait, bucket, nets. While he is getting ready, he gets very excited. Then he sits by the sea without saying a word for hours, totally focused, oblivious to the world. He looks like a Buddhist monk in a kind of a meditative trance. Fishing makes him relaxed and happy.

But it is not quite the innocent sport it seems. Fish have to be killed. Like all fishermen, Jelisić must have loved the moment when he tugged the line and felt that he had a catch. The fish would appear from the water, wriggling helplessly on the hook. I can imagine him unhooking the fish and throwing it on the grass. Then watching it gasp for air. But perhaps it wasn't like that at all. There are other ways of dealing with fish. If he catches a big fish, a fisherman will usually put a thumb into its mouth and break its neck with an unpleasant, snapping sound. Or he may throw it in a bucket of water and postpone its end. Maybe Goran was gentle: maybe this is what he did with his fish.

If someone had asked him how he would have liked to spend his life, Goran would not have hesitated much before answering. But nobody ever asked him what he wanted, and he knew that life was not about fishing. To him, perhaps, it seemed as though people were the fish, big or small, catching and eating each other, and he did not want to be eaten.

Later – after he had left Luka – he would come to the river and just lie there, wishing that it was spring again and that nothing had happened. Sometimes it worked.

One of the witnesses for the defence was the president of the local fishing club. This man could not accept what Jelisić did in Brčko. It did not tally with the image of him as a fisherman. The way he knew Jelisić, sitting on a bank of the Sava River, staring at the water or just sunbathing while occasionally looking at the rod and waiting for a fish to bite – this was not consistent with the brutality described at the Tribunal. He vouched that Jelisić was a nice, quiet man, somebody who would certainly never hurt a fly, let alone another person. He said so many nice things about Jelisić that one of the judges angrily reproached him, saying that his moral principles came second to friendship and fishing expeditions. But the man was not impressed. 'It is my job to have a professional attitude towards all fishermen,' he said.

Goran Jelisić grew up in a working-class family in the small town of Bijeljina, which was about 40 per cent Muslim. His mother worked, so he was brought up by his grandmother. He grew up in a street where Serbs and Muslims lived side by side, and many friends of his family were Muslims. They all played together, went to school together, to bars, to football matches. He did not pay any attention to their Muslim nationality, nor they to his Serbian one. He was never heard to utter an offensive word about anyone. His neighbours say that he was well brought up and well behaved. He was a good and loyal friend. In the late eighties, he did not take Serbian nationalism seriously. He did not pay much attention to the idea that Serbs should all live in one state, and, anyway, politics was for politicians. It had nothing to do with his life, with his friends and fishing. But he turned out to be wrong.

When he finished school, Goran got a job as a farm mechanic. It was not a good job, but at least it was a job at a time when most of his friends were unemployed. He was not pleased about making so little money. If only he had money, he could do something with his life, be independent, start a small business, perhaps even leave Bijeljina, although he would miss it. He had an idea how to make money: by forging cheques. For that, he was sentenced to a year and half in prison.

Jelisić appeared as a character witness for Esad Landjo in the so-called 'Ćelebići case'. He explained at length to the judges how good a person Esad Landjo was and how he helped other prisoners in the Scheveningen prison, for example by teaching them how to work with a computer, cooking for them, or advising them on how to behave in prison. In fact, Landjo (a Muslim) was another war criminal whose alleged speciality was setting Serbian prisoners of war on fire. Jelisić's voice was pleasant, and nothing about him suggested that he himself might be one of the accused.

Even now, in a courtroom, I could not help but see Goran as one of my daughter's generation. Nothing in his life had prepared him for war. He had served several months in prison for cheque fraud and, when he got out in February 1992, it was because Republika Srpska was implementing a strategy to provide volunteers for the war by releasing prisoners. Jelisić volunteered for the police and in May was sent to a Brčko police station. This was the beginning of his downfall. But I think he became a volunteer policeman not because he was eager to kill and had long suppressed the desire, but because it was hard to avoid becoming one. Perhaps he did not even know what being a volunteer actually meant. However, once he was there, in that Brčko police station, it was another matter.

Of course, if someone had testified that he had taken pleasure in seeing fish suffer, it would at least have been a small sign that Jelisić had a bad character long before he ended up beating and killing prisoners. But his fishing friends said nothing of the sort. There is, in fact, nothing pathological about his life and behaviour before the war. The image of him drawn by the witnesses for his defence makes you wonder if they are really describing the person on trial for murder.

According to them, Jelisić was a good and faithful friend, ready to take risks in order to help people. The Tribunal found itself caught up in a very peculiar situation: as the defence lawyer pointed out, never before had there been a case where so many people from a victimised ethnic group acted as witnesses on behalf of a Serbian defendant.

People who came to defend him, his neighbours, friends and schoolmates – many of them Muslims, including the president of the fishermen's club – all said that they could not believe that he had committed those murders, even those aware that he had admitted to it. They knew Jelisić as a different man – as a fisherman.

He was quiet and shy, one witness said, and he was known to help everybody: he helped at least seven or eight families in a single street during the war. Another witness remembered how Jelisić helped an old Muslim woman whose windows had shattered when a bomb exploded in her yard by paying for the repair. A good friend of many years, also a Muslim, told the judges what Jelisić did for him and his family during and after the war. Not only did he give money to his wife while the friend was in captivity, but he also later helped them cross the border to Serbia so they could flee abroad. Jelisić also helped his friend's sister and her husband to escape in the same way after the war. When the warlord Željko Ražnatović Arkan's paramilitary forces threatened to kill another of his Muslim friends in Bijeljina, Jelisić saved him and his wife, and his mother even spent a few days in Jelisić's house with his parents. And he saved the life of his friend's son when he needed an emergency spleen operation. It was Jelisić who took him to the hospital and covered all expenses. Another person described him as a 'nice and honest boy', and a female friend said that he was 'a very well brought up child, on the streets, at school, at home. His behaviour was always good.'

Why, then, did this nice fisherman ended up executing Muslim prisoners?

I have two photographs in front of me, two very famous photographs that were published all over the world. They are images of a uniformed man executing a prisoner. They are comparable to the brutal photograph from the Vietnam War that shows the Saigon police chief shooting a Vietcong soldier through the head at close range. The only difference seems to be that this execution took place in Bosnia some thirty years later, on 7 May 1992. The executioner wears a policeman's uniform and his back is turned to the photographer. He is aiming his pistol at the head of a prisoner who is walking about a metre in front of him, his head bent down, aware that he might get a bullet at any moment. In the next photograph the prisoner has been shot in the back of his head. At the Tribunal, Jelisić admitted that he had fired the gun.

But what exactly had gone through his mind before that, before Jelisić raised his arm and fired the bullet that would decide not only the fate of the prisoner in the photograph, but his own as well? For after that single shot, there was no way back for Jelisić. On that day in May, he started out on a road which, six years later, would bring him to the Tribunal in The Hague. What happens to a human being that makes him kill another human being in cold blood? Jelisić killed randomly, arbitrarily, and he seems to have enjoyed it. According to the prosecution, he acted like the 'willing executioner'. Without such enthusiasts, no ethnic cleansing would be possible, said the prosecutor. But neither the prosecution nor the defence could offer the smallest clue about how he became an executioner.

Jelisić was twenty-three when he executed the prisoner in the photograph. But could Jelisić's face lie so much? I wondered, looking at this young man in the courtroom. Absolutely nothing about his appearance suggested a violent nature, neither his looks nor his manners, not even the way he expressed himself. Or perhaps . . . well, he had the habit of jiggling one leg nervously under the desk, while sitting in the courtroom with a perfectly calm expression on his face. He would jiggle it constantly. Was this a sign of pathology? What was his true nature? Perhaps being a fisherman was in fact closer to his true nature? While he was in the Scheveningen prison awaiting trial, two psychiatrists were called in to evaluate him. Their report suggested that he had an antisocial personality, was narcissistic, immature and longing for recognition. In their opinion, this made him a borderline personality – bordering on perversity, that is. The experts, Dr Van den Bussche and Dr Duits, used expressions such as 'repugnant', 'bestial' and 'sadistic nature' to describe his behaviour towards the prisoners at the Luka camp. The judges sentencing him concluded, in their summing up, that he indeed had a disturbed personality.

Surviving prisoners who came to The Hague as witnesses did not use such strong words as the psychiatrists, or offer pronouncements on the character of Goran Jelisić. But several of them described his eyes: 'He had very high cheekbones too, and his eyes were somehow unnaturally expressive, like turbid water,' one witness said. 'He seemed to have been using some stimulants or something like that. Whoever met his eyes, I think, would avoid looking at him again. I think he installed [sic] a kind of fear with his look, especially after he had introduced himself. I don't really know how to put it . . . I mean our fear, which was already very great, I think, tripled after the look we received from him. That is perhaps how I could put it best.' Another man, the witness F, described his look as powerful and cruel. His eyes did not laugh, only his mouth. 'I used to see that kind of thing in films,' F said.

'Hitler was the first Adolf, I am the second,' Jelisić used to introduce himself to prisoners. In the Luka camp near Brčko, they trembled on hearing his voice, because it quite literally meant death. He would enter the hangar where the prisoners were kept and pick out victims at random, just by saying 'you, you and you'. No names were called out, no accusations or verdicts offered. First he would collect the prisoners' money, watches and jewellery. Often, he beat them. He would do this in front of his girlfriend, Monika, who sometimes visited the camp because her brother was in charge of it. Then the prisoners were forced to come out of the hangar, one by one. Jelisić would tell a man to kneel down and place his head over a metal drainage grating. Then he would execute him with two bullets in the back of the head using a pistol with a silencer. For a minute or two before the execution, the man he had chosen would plead for his life: 'Don't do this to me. Why me? I haven't done anything.' But it would not help him. Before killing him Jelisić would curse his Muslim mother. Indeed, the more fear the victim showed, the more pleasure Jelisić took in killing him. Afterwards, two prisoners would take the body to a refrigerated truck used to drive bodies to a mass grave. Then Jelisić would order the blood to be cleaned from the grating. He hated untidiness.

When he was in a good mood, Jelisić would explain how nice it was to kill. 'I can see that you are scared. It is nice to kill people this way. I kill them nicely. I don't feel anything.' Prisoners from the Luka camp who were witnesses at the Tribunal remember how he killed a tall, strong prisoner, a Croat. First he cut off the man's ear. Then he walked him back to the hangar for others to see him. Holding his own ear in his hand, the man pleaded with the prisoners to kill him, and not to give Jelisić that pleasure. Jelisić took his pistol out and offered it to the prisoners, urging them to kill the man. But nobody volunteered. Jelisić sneered at them, telling them they were not worthy of being allowed to live. In the end, he executed the tall Croat by the grating, the same way he had the others.

Merely by pointing his finger, he decided whether someone lived or died. He executed old men as well as young ones. He killed an eighteen-year-old Muslim girl. He killed an old man because he dropped a bottle of water and a young man because he was married to a Serbian woman. And he kept repeating his score loudly: sixty-eight, seventy-nine, eighty-three ... Allegedly, he single-handedly executed more than a hundred prisoners in eighteen days in May 1992. He bragged that he had to kill twenty to thirty people before he took his morning coffee. He was sentenced because his killing of thirteen of them was proven.

Jelisić might have been a nice guy to his friends and neighbours, and he was undoubtedly a good fisherman. But he was also a killer, as he himself admitted. In fact he was one of three people (out of more than sixty) accused of war crimes who admitted their crimes in front of the Tribunal, who said 'I am guilty' on thirty-one counts – and yet did not show any real remorse. Although the majority of people he murdered were Muslims, the judges concluded that there was not enough evidence to find Jelisić guilty of genocide – that is, for having had the systematic, conscious intention of wiping out Muslims. They claimed that, because of the perverse features of his character, Jelisić would probably have willingly killed members of any ethnic group. Therefore the charge of genocide was dropped, and Jelisić was sentenced to forty years in prison for violations of the laws or customs of war as well as for crimes against humanity.

The defence correctly pointed out that Jelisić acted as an executioner only during those eighteen days in May – not before and not after. How was it possible, his lawyers asked, that this man turned into a monster for only eighteen days? According to them, the only rational explanation was that he was acting under pressure, that he was killing on command. He was obeying orders and was afraid for his own life.

This could indeed have been the case. It would fit well with his love of fishing and the calm, benevolent disposition that he usually displayed. But, since there was not enough evidence to sustain the claim that he obeyed orders, the Tribunal ruled that the opposite was the case and that Jelisić executed prisoners of his own free will.

However, there was more than enough evidence of something else. Several prisoners said that Jelisić obviously enjoyed executing people: he showed off by keeping count, he explained his methods, he explicitly stated that he liked what he was doing. These witnesses also said that the more a man would plead for his life, the more pleasure Jelisić would take in executing him. Evidently, it was not the act of killing itself that he liked.

What did happen, then, during those eighteen crucial days? Nobody could explain for certain, not even Jelisić himself.

Perhaps what had changed was not the person, but the circumstances. There was no longer peace; there was war now. Jelisić could no longer find the opportunity to lie in the grass while the river gently murmured and the world around him stood still. The war changed it all. My son-in-law, too, had to leave behind fishing in his beloved Adriatic when he left for Canada at about the same time as Goran Jelisić left for Brčko. The war changed both their lives, but in very different ways. How much of that change was due to a conscious decision, how much to coincidence? Why did one of them leave for Canada and the other for Brčko? Could it have been the other way around? Could my son-in-law have become a volunteer in the Croatian police instead? I believe that he could not. But why could he not, while Jelisić could? I don't know the answer. There are many people who seem to be perfectly normal, but under certain conditions, as in those that prevail in wartime, their pathological side comes to the fore and dominates their behaviour. Could it be that Jelisić always had a pathological side that surfaced only when the conditions permitted?

For the first time in his short life, Goran Jelisić was in a position of power. A little man from Bijeljina, a farm mechanic and petty criminal just out of prison, a fisherman, a nobody – he suddenly had absolute power. He was given a pistol and the freedom to use it, and he became intoxicated by the new possibilities. People said he looked and behaved as if he was on drugs. His eyes were strange and he was agitated, nervous. Perhaps having power over someone else's life and death is the strongest drug of all. To the prisoners, he was like a god. He got high on showing off his power by executing prisoners, that nice looking young man, Goran, one of my daughter's generation.

But I keep thinking that even if he did become an executioner, in a deeper sense he was a victim himself. Goran Jelisić and his entire generation were cheated. Many of his parents' generation – my generation – embraced the nationalist ideology and did nothing to prevent the war that grew out of it. They were too opportunistic and too frightened not to follow the leaders they had learned to follow. And many of their children paid for their parents' stupidity, sometimes with their own lives. Even a killer who might spend the rest of his life in prison, like Goran Jelisić.

7

'Triumph of Evil'

General Radislav Krstić, commander of the forces of Republika Srpska and the deputy commander of the Drina Corps, was the first war criminal sentenced for genocide by the Tribunal in The Hague. He was sentenced to forty-six years in prison for crimes committed in the UN-safe area of Srebrenica between 13 and 19 July 1995, when more than seven thousand Muslim men were executed, while thirty thousand people were forcibly deported. His adjutant major, Dragan Obrenović, was sentenced to seventeen years in prison in December 2003..

General Radislav Krstić looked worried as he entered the courtroom limping slightly; like many, he had personally paid the price of this war, having lost his leg when he stepped on a mine in December 1994. A slim man of fifty wearing a dark jacket, he had combed his greyish, thinning hair over his nearly bald head, a sign of his vanity.

Seated hunched behind a desk, a worried frown on his

forehead, he threw nervous glances at the judges. I got the impression that he felt uneasy in this place, amid lawyers and judges dressed up in solemn black and red robes as though for a theatrical performance. But here, unlike in a theatre, the drama being played out was genuine and deadly serious. From the very beginning of his trial, which lasted more than a year, Krstić wore that same expression of anxiety on his face. He looked like a trapped man, a weak man, a man full of fears.

As I sat in the courtroom watching him, I remembered a brief scene from a documentary about Republika Srpska forces entering Srebrenica on the afternoon of 11 July 1995. The scene shows General Ratko Mladić, Commander-in-Chief of the Serbian forces, ordering his soldiers to take the enclave. General Mladić, Krstić's immediate superior, summons him not by his title or by his full name, but by his nickname, Krle, as if they are at some private party. 'Krle, come here!' Mladić barks, in the same way he would summon a waiter or call a dog to heel. Looking down at the ground in front of him, Krstić follows him, though not very willingly. This short scene, to me, sums up their relationship: that of an aggressive, domineering master and his submissive servant. A relationship for which Krstić will have to pay with forty-six years in gaol.

In his opening statement, the prosecutor, Mark Harmon, said: 'This is a case about the triumph of evil, a story about how officers and soldiers of the Bosnian Serb Army – men who professed to be professional soldiers, men who professed to represent the ideals of a distinguished Serbian past – organised, planned and willingly participated in genocide or stood silent in the face of it. The authors of these foul deeds have left a legacy that has stained the reputation of the Serbian people and has disgraced the honourable profession of arms.'

But this was not so clear-cut when the trial started. My first impression of Krstić – the way he talked, the tone of his voice, the consideration he showed when he listened to the testimony of victims and the air of naiveté about him – was not of a man who could have taken part in such horrible deeds as the mass executions of Muslim men from Srebrenica. He looked anxious and frightened, not like a vicious bully poisoned by hatred and hungry for revenge. Even in the documentary, which showed him in uniform and standing next to General Mladić in Srebrenica, he didn't strike me as a military man in the same way that Mladić did; he didn't look at all like an aggressive person. He seemed too silent, too withdrawn and too intellectual, more like an army bureaucrat content to shuffle papers at his desk rather than lead soldiers into battle. The image he wanted to convey in front of the Tribunal was that of a person of integrity, that of a professional soldier.

Krstić reminds me of my father, who ended up as a professional soldier right after the Second World War was over. Becoming an officer in the victorious army of Tito's partisans was a good career opportunity for him, certainly better than being demobilised and having to go back to his old job as a carpenter. But I always thought of my father as more of a white-collar worker, with an appetite for elegant clothes, good food and dances at the Officers' Club – things that would make a real soldier go soft. And indeed, at the end of his military career, he was just doing paperwork and because of his bad health took early retirement. This is exactly what Krstić would have done, if it hadn't been for the war.

My father's uniform always smelled of a mixture of tobacco and vinegar. It was back in the early fifties, and he probably only had one uniform. I remember how my mother would iron it every Sunday afternoon on the kitchen table, while my father listened to a football match on the radio, his head bent close to the set. Mother would pour water into a metal bowl and add a few drops of red wine vinegar to it. That will freshen up the colour, she used to say. Then she would dip a thin piece of cloth into the bowl, wring it out and smooth it over the trousers laid out on the table. She would heat up the heavy black iron on the stove, then press it firmly on to the cloth, and each time she did a cloud of steam would rise, hissing, from the table. Father's uniform would always be perfectly ironed, but every time I kissed him I smelled that pungent odour.

Without his uniform, my father was quite a different man, as if he had been deprived of his power. Suddenly, he was smaller, somehow weaker and quieter. I thought of this as I watched Krstić sitting there in the courtroom in his dark blue blazer, looking lost. His uniform seemed to have given him his identity, and I even wondered if his uniform had had that same unforgettable smell as my father's, that reminded me of his different selves. It must have been very humiliating for him to sit there dressed as a simple civilian.

Because he reminded me so much of my father, I had a hard time remembering that Krstić is a man of my generation, not of my father's. When I heard that he had been arrested by UN forces in 1998, I did not even realise this immediately, because I did not know anyone from my generation who had joined the army. It was not a profession that the young men I knew had ever considered. We were city kids, studying fancy subjects like philosophy, art history or psychology at the Philosophical Faculty of the Zagreb University.

But it was different for someone born in a remote Bosnian village. Becoming a professional soldier might be the only way out of such a village, especially if his parents were poor peasants. A uniform would guarantee a hot meal, proper clothes, a pair of shoes, free accommodation, salary and one less mouth for his parents to feed. There is enormous respect for a uniform in any such village. A uniform, any uniform, means power, and power is respected and feared. And even for the supposedly egalitarian Yugoslav society, becoming an officer has always meant rising in status.

There were many reasons for young Radislav Krstić to become an officer. In addition to getting out into the world, an officer would be decently paid and, if he got married, could get an apartment. From the point of view of those of us who were his peers, this was a big advantage. As snobbish as we were, we had to go on living with our parents in their apartment, even after we got married and had babies. Having our own apartment was beyond our dreams. We could not afford to rent one for ourselves. But in spite of their advantages, we all knew that, under their uniforms, Krstić and other young men like him were different from us. Under their uniforms they were still country boys, scared and out of place in the city. And, although Krstić's wife must certainly have used an electric iron to iron his uniform, rather than one she had to heat up on the stove, he seemed to belong both to my father's generation and to mine.

But there were plenty of things that identified him as part of my generation: growing up with the cult of Tito's personality, the glorification of the partisan struggle against fascism, the communist revolution during the Second World War, and, most important, the ruling ideology of 'brotherhood and unity' (*bratstvo i jedinstvo*), that is, of different nations living happily together in a common Yugoslavia. In that sense, Krstić's childhood and youth in his small village were probably not so different from mine in the city. In Vlasenica and Han Pijesak, where Krstić went to school, he would have learned from textbooks similar to the ones I had to read. We grew up hearing the same stories, like the one about young Tito preparing a smoked pig's head for his little brothers and sisters (who got diarrhoea afterwards), and the one about Boško Buha, the young partisan courier who became a hero. We learned all the partisan offensives by heart. Sometime in the early sixties Krstić and his class from school probably visited the battle site of Sutjeska at Tjentište, or the Ustashe concentration camp in Jasenovac, just as I did with my class. They sang the same patriotic songs as we did. School children used to watch mandatory movies about the partisans – about the battles of Neretva and Kozara and the attack on Drvar. Every 25 May, the 'Day of Youth' and Tito's birthday, the young Krstić probably sat beside his radio, listening to the celebrations in a sports stadium in Belgrade: the arrival of relay runners in Tito's honour, the spectacular gymnastics display. Later, he and his family probably enjoyed the TV series *Pozorište u kući* (*Theatre at Home*) and laughed at its popular comic actor Čkalja. They ate *sarma* on New Year's Eve. I can even imagine that his first car was a small Fiat 750, nicknamed *Fićo*, and that he spent his summer holidays in Brela or Makarska on the Adriatic coast.

But neither he nor I ever thought that one day it would be different. Yugoslavia seemed so safe. Brotherhood and unity seemed so real. We grew up together, went to school together – Serbs and Croats and Muslims – befriended each other, got married, had children, never thinking that nationality could be something that would split us apart. The only exceptions were the Albanians. The few of them who lived in Croatia worked mostly as goldsmiths or in ice-cream parlours. In Serbia, they did the dirtiest and most poorly paid jobs. It was difficult to mix with them, not because of the language barrier – most of them spoke Serbo-Croatian – but because of their low social status. We looked upon them as people who came from an altogether different and inferior world.

In his opening remarks at the Tribunal, speaking about his life, Krstić confirmed that '... never had there been any incidents, anything that would have been caused by national intolerance. Quite the contrary. We all went to school together, we socialised together and we had great respect for each other. This applied also to the elderly population of the village, but it applied in particular to the younger generation.' I knew what Krstić meant; I could have said the same thing. I remember my school pals from Serbia, Macedonia and Bosnia, with their strange names and strange dialects. We were aware of the differences, of course, but they did not bother us at all.

Apart from school, the army was one of the government's ways of creating 'brotherhood and unity'. Young conscripts were sent far away from home to get acquainted with their country. The Yugoslav National Army (JNA) was considered to be the people's army and 'the biggest school of brotherhood and unity', one of the very guarantees of statehood. It is a truly terrible paradox of the war that the same army that had the important role of building brotherhood and unity among the peoples of Yugoslavia turned into the main instrument used against it.

The urge to overcome traditional national divisions was revealed in a census held in 1981 in which some 1.2 million people declared themselves to be 'Yugoslavs'. This group was the sixth largest 'nation' in Yugoslavia at that time and consisted mostly of people of the post-war generation, many of them urban professionals and from mixed marriages. This might have been the beginning of a Yugoslav melting pot, except that it did not work. We did not all become Yugoslavs.

When he spoke about his past, especially about the nine years he spent in Sarajevo, from 1972 to 1981, General Krstić sounded nostalgic, almost romantic. He got married, had a daughter and lived in his own apartment. 'Those were beautiful years of my life,' Krstić said. But there was something about Sarajevo that he especially appreciated, something that other cities in Yugoslavia did not have. 'This spirit of unity was particularly pronounced in the town of Sarajevo. We never inquired about each other's ethnic backgrounds. We all felt like residents of Sarajevo,' he observed, perhaps forgetting for a moment that he was in a courtroom and that his words might sound unconvincing to the judges and the audience.

In 1991 the war started, first in Slovenia, then in Croatia. The break-up of Yugoslavia was painful and horrible for Krstić, as he acknowledged at the Tribunal. Indeed, it must have been distressing for him to see how everything that he believed in went down the drain. In those years I thought a lot about my father – he had died in November 1989 – and how the changes would have affected him. I would not have wanted him to see Yugoslavia falling apart because of the nationalism that he fought against all his life. I would not have wanted him to see a partisan general turn into a pro-fascist politician, like Franjo Tudjman, who came to power in Croatia. This must have been confusing and frightening for Krstić: he was not a man of politics and, as he himself said, he had underestimated the role politics played in bringing the war about.

But Krstić still believed that Bosnia would not succumb to war. Like the majority of Bosnians, he was convinced that war could not occur in such an ethnically mixed country. Here I would have agreed with him. I was in Sarajevo, too, and I felt the same relaxed, tolerant atmosphere there. Even when the war had started in Croatia, people in Sarajevo used to say, 'Nobody could divide us. Muslims, Serbs and Croats live here on the same floor of apartment buildings.' There was no history of ethnic clashes over the last forty-five years, and one-third of the children came from mixed marriages. Nevertheless, in April 1992, war came to Bosnia.

That year Krstić was in Priština. Around him officers of non-Serbian background were leaving the Yugoslav National Army corps. Finally, in the middle of that year, after Bosnia had proclaimed independence, Krstić understood that it was his turn to choose where he wanted to live: in Serbia or in Bosnia. He decided on Bosnia, where he was born. But when he arrived there, he saw that it had become deeply divided among Serbs, Croats and Muslims. He was a Serb, and perhaps for the first time he was in the position to realise fully the implications of this. For him, as for so many others, his nationality became his destiny. So, in June 1992 and with the war already raging, he joined the armed forces of Republika Srpska.

So far I could follow him: I could see how his life had unfolded, and I could understand his disappointments, his confusion, his naiveté and his fears. I could also understand his trust in politicians; in a communist country, politicians were the ones who were supposed to solve problems. Krstić was convinced that the politicians had to find a solution, and in this he was not alone. People placed so much faith in a political solution that they did not see through a politician like Slobodan Milošević. The country was falling apart, and Milošević's only goal was to stay in power – even if the price was war. The Serbian media stirred people into a nationalist fervour, spreading propaganda until Serbs in both Serbia and Bosnia were utterly convinced that they were threatened by the 'Others'. The Croatian and Bosnian media soon joined the frenzy. Vukovar was destroyed, Dubrovnik was shelled, Sarajevo was besieged – and still Krstić harboured some naive hope that there could be a political solution to the Bosnian situation.

As I looked at Krstić in the courtroom, there were moments, I admit, when I felt sorry for him. I thought about what he had said and what he had not said, but I especially thought about a question that nobody had asked him, although it seems to me to be the most important one: how was it possible that a person who grew up without ethnic prejudices, a professional officer who was educated in the Yugoslav National Army in the spirit of 'brotherhood and unity', could end up being accused of genocide against his Muslim neighbours? If he was really so ethnically unbiased, if he enjoyed ethnically mixed Sarajevo so much, why did he support the nationalist politics of Republika Srpska? How did he find himself in a situation whereby he was ordering the killing of people whom, only yesterday, he had been protecting? How could any person of even basic integrity do that?

Perhaps Krstić acted against all his instincts, behaved contrary to everything that he had ever learned and loved, in effect denied his very self. But this could have cost him his sanity. Perhaps he convinced himself that he had to save his own life and that he could also act in defence of his own people. Once the war started, people had to choose, they had to take sides. Sometimes this meant splitting up a family. Krstić's situation was dramatic, but no more so than anybody else's. If people did not want to take sides, they often had to leave the country. There were many such cases. There were also people of different nationalities who continued living together throughout the war, especially in Sarajevo. But the majority did take sides, and for Krstić, a professional soldier, this meant joining the armed forces of Republika Srpska.

At this point, at the beginning of the war in Bosnia, this man who loved Sarajevo so much did not choose to return there. Perhaps this was because it was besieged, but perhaps it was also because he no longer felt like a Sarajevan. With his peasant background he preferred a village, where he felt safer.

Sarajevans used to say that the war in Bosnia was a war of peasants against city dwellers, with the former led by people like Radovan Karadžić, who was from a small village in Montenegro and understood little of urban life. Such a man never really fitted into Sarajevo and felt humiliated by its citizens – but now he had his chance to take revenge.

Once Krstić decided to join the Republika Srpska forces, what happened to him thereafter was more or less determined by circumstance. During the next three years he was promoted several times, the last when he was made Lieutenant General and Deputy Chief of Staff of the Drina Corps. A month later, in July 1995, the Drina Corps was given an assignment in the towns of Srebrenica and Žepa. At the same time the Chief of Staff of the Republika Srpska troops, General Ratko Mladić, took over command in Srebrenica. For Krstić this was an ominous moment, when his compliant character 'allowed' him to choose the wrong side, when he 'agreed to evil', as the prosecutor Mark Harmon put it. This was the moment when he should have resisted the forces of circumstance – assuming, of course, that Krstić was indeed against the deportation and extermination of Muslims. In fact, Krstić could not resist these forces; he did not have the strength. He was an opportunist who went with the tide. In the three years since he had joined the armed forces of Republika Srpska, he had come to the point where he could no longer refuse to obey orders from General Mladić. But, during his time in Srebrenica, he must at least have been aware of the consequences.

I do not believe that Krstić is a pathological case, an evil man who hated Muslims and wanted to destroy them. But he does strike me as somebody who struggles with himself. He is a weak man, a man who is afraid to say no to a higher authority. This happened to thousands of others, too. This 'policy of small steps', of everyday decisions and concessions, of a collaboration on a much smaller scale, brought men like Krstić into situations where they had either to obey or disobey the orders of men like Ratko Mladić. In Krstić's case, the order was to kill the Muslims from Srebrenica. Krstić could have disobeyed Mladić. He could have resigned or issued a counter order. Instead, he decided to do nothing. Opposing Mladić would have proved too costly for him, as he tried to explain to the Tribunal: 'Not in my wildest dreams was I able to undertake any measures. We weren't allowed to talk about anything like that, let alone take steps against a commanding officer, regardless of my knowledge that he or somebody else had perhaps committed a war crime.' The only justification for going along that he offered the judges was his own cowardice.

The fact is that Krstić did not object when Mladić took over the command of his troops and started issuing orders; he remained silent when Mladić threatened to exterminate people in Srebrenica. Although Krstić claimed that he did not know about the mass executions, it seems unlikely that he would have done anything to stop them if he had known. Indeed, by the time the executions started, it was too late to do anything. Mladić's authority was too great. An officer does not challenge his superiors, and especially not if he had previously served in the Yugoslav National Army. Every army is, by definition, an authoritarian institution, but a communist army even more so, and Mladić was not a person one could oppose without fearing the consequences. Radislav Krstić admitted that he was scared of Ratko Mladić, both while they were in Srebrenica and after what happened there. Several times during his cross-examination, Krstić said that he had feared for his family and for himself. The judges, however, seemed unimpressed. In their eyes this was not an excuse. There are such things as rules of war, ethics of war and an officer's honour, and it was Krstić's duty to respect those values and to prevent war crimes. If he couldn't, he should have reported it. He didn't. Not knowing about the crimes while they were taking place should not have prevented him from reporting them the moment he found out about them. But to whom? To his superiors, Mladić and Karadžić? Or to UNPROFOR (the United Nations Protection Force)? In all fairness, we do have to stop here and think: what could Krstić have possibly done?

On the other hand, perhaps the idea of individual responsibility was simply too abstract for General Krstić to understand. After all, where would he have learned about it? Communist society, like the nationalist one that replaced it, is a collective society; there is no such thing as individual responsibility because there is very little individualism.

Still, we must ask ourselves: how does our neighbour become our enemy? How do we internalise the enemy, and how long does it take to do so? By the time the enclave of Srebrenica fell, the Serbian propaganda machine, especially television, had been demonising the enemy for almost ten years – that is, Croats, Bosnian Muslims and Albanians. Srebrenica's fall and the mass executions following it were made possible only because of the long psychological preparation. By 1995, the Muslims had become a non-people, much like the Jews during the Second World War. The extermination of Jews also began with small steps. Little things, such as not being allowed to buy flowers in a local shop, to have your hair cut at the hairdresser, or to ride a tram, eventually led them to the gas chamber.

In Bosnia numerous war crimes had been committed before 1995, by participants on all sides of the conflict, and all in the name of nationalism. The offensive on the Srebrenica enclave was apparently in retaliation for an earlier attack undertaken by Bosnian Muslim forces on the neighbouring Serbian village of Kravice, in which many Serbian civilians were killed.

Hence, perhaps, killing Muslims was justified in the eyes of the perpetrators, including Krstić himself. But what took place in Srebrenica was not just a military operation – with some 'collateral damage' – but a deliberate act of 'ethnic cleansing'. More than seven thousand men were summarily executed, while some thirty thousand women, children and elderly people were forcibly deported in a concerted effort to rid the Drina valley area of its entire Muslim population. This was done according to the instructions of the President of Republika Srpska, Radovan Karadžić, to 'create an unbearable situation of total insecurity with no hope of future survival or life for the inhabitants of Srebrenica and Žepa'.

Sometimes, amazingly, there is at least one person who manages to survive a mass execution. One of them, a witness at the Tribunal known as 'O', took the stand at the Krstić trial to tell about the biggest mass killing in Europe since the Second World War. He was just seventeen when it happened: 'Some people shouted, "Give us some water first, then kill us." I was really sorry that I would die thirsty and I was trying to hide amongst the people as long as I could, like everybody else. I just wanted to live for another second or two. And when it was my turn, I jumped out with what I believe were four other people. I was walking with my head bent down and I wasn't feeling anything . . . I saw rows of killed people. It looked like they had been lined up, one row after the other. And then I thought that I would die very fast, that I would not suffer. And I just thought that my mother would never know where I had ended up.'

As the young man called witness 'O' was speaking at the Tribunal, Krstić seemed visibly shaken by his words. He did not know where to look. This underscored even more my impression of his compassion for his victims. He appeared to find it almost unbearable to listen to this witness, as if this one young man, who should have been one of the seven thousand murdered, who had survived to tell about it only by chance, finally brought home to Krstić the reality of his deeds. But then the prosecutor started to cross-examine him. And then my perception of Radislav Krstić changed drastically.

Krstić's line of defence was a simple one. He did not deny that war crimes had been committed by Republika Srpska units, but he denied issuing orders for these crimes. General Mladić outranked him and always took command. Krstić argued that Mladić overruled him and issued orders himself, directly to the battalion commanders. Day after day, during cross-examination, he tried to convince the prosecutor and the judges that he had nothing to do with the entire operation. In other words, Krstić's strategy was one of complete denial. He denied not only participating in the planning, organising or ordering of killings and deportations, but also of even knowing they were happening. Moreover, he declared, he was not there at the time. From the afternoon of 12 July, he was in Žepa and heard nothing about what was going on in Srebrenica. In fact, he said, he first learned about most of the atrocities at his own trial.

He frequently answered the prosecutor's questions with 'I don't know', even when it sounded highly improbable, even when he must have known. For example, as early as 17 July 1995, an adviser to Radovan Karadžić publicly denied accusations concerning the torture, killing and deportation of Muslim civilians in Srebrenica, claiming they were treated well by the Serbs. Reports in the world press about the suspicion of war crimes committed in Srebrenica appeared very early, and even the official Chinese news agency had written about them by 17 July. But no, General Krstić had heard nothing.

When the prosecutor asked him if, while driving towards Potočari, he had seen any of the many buses and trucks that had been dispatched to transport people out of the enclave, Krstić said he had not noticed them. These events happened in an area of some forty square kilometres, and Krstić actually gave an interview on camera with a number of parked buses in the background. It was like the deputy mayor of a small town saying he hadn't noticed a big football match going on in his town, or the convoy of fifty or sixty buses, or the thousands of football fans in the streets, or the traffic jams and policemen everywhere . . .

As the prosecutor showed, it was simply impossible for a person in Krstić's position not to notice what was happening around him. Deporting thirty thousand people and killing seven thousand – that would be a very big and difficult logistical operation. It would have to involve the cooperation, knowledge and participation of countless soldiers, as prosecutor Peter McCloskey pointed out at the trial: 'First, it involved the issuing, the transmitting and the dissemination of orders to all units that participated in the movement, the killing, the burial and reburial of the victims. It involved the assembling of a sufficient number of vehicles and buses, trucks, to transport the thousands of victims from the location of their capture and surrender to detention centres that were located near the execution sites. It involved obtaining fuel for these vehicles – providing guards and security for each of the vehicles – identifying detention centres that were secure enough and in close proximity to the execution fields. It involved obtaining sufficient numbers of blindfolds and ligatures so these prisoners could be bound before they were executed – sufficient men to secure the actual detention facilities themselves, to guard the prisoners for the days or for the hours that they were kept there before they were executed; obtaining transportation; organising the killing squads and arming the killing squads; the requisitioning and transportation of heavy-duty equipment necessary to dig the large mass graves and it required men to bury the thousands of victims whom we were later to discover.' In September that same year, 1995, the mass graves were dug up and the bodies were transferred to a variety of distant locations. Even if he was in Žepa, General Krstić was fully aware of what was happening. It was his officers and soldiers from the Drina Corps who participated in this systematic operation, including the cover-up.

At the Tribunal Krstić was obviously lying, and doing so very unconvincingly. But he didn't seem to be lying in order to get a reduced sentence, because he already knew that he would be sentenced not only for his individual accountability but also for his responsibility as a commander. More likely, he lied in the futile belief that with all the blame for Srebrenica falling on Mladić, he could save his own face and self-respect. But there could be another reason. In his own mind, his responsibility could be proved only if he was caught with the smoking gun in his hand. Besides, in Bosnia, Serbia or Croatia, one does not necessarily have to be ashamed of lying. I remember how astonished Western ambassadors, politicians and envoys invariably were after meetings with Mladić, Karadžić or Milošević: looking straight into Lord Owen's, Carl Bildt's or Richard Holbrooke's eyes, these men would lie, give their word of honour and sign treaties they never thought twice about upholding. It took some time before foreigners from the West realised that. Life in post-communist societies – as well as in communist ones – is immersed in a culture of lies. There is no moral code that admonishes, 'Thou Shalt Not Lie!' On the contrary, anyone can see with his own eyes that by lying one survives and profits, and that telling the truth is stupid.

If there was ever a chance for Krstić to convince the prosecution, the judges and the public of the truthfulness of what he said, to make them believe that he was a professional officer and a man of integrity, it was irrevocably lost when McCloskey produced a tape recording of an intercepted conversation between Krstić and his adjutant major, Dragan Obrenović. Before playing the tape, McCloskey asked, 'General Krstić, did you ever order the killing of Muslims?' Vehemently, Krstić answered, 'No!' Then McCloskey played the tape, and it become clear why he had asked the question.

Krstić: Are you working down there?

Obrenović: Of course we're working.

Krstić: Good.

Obrenović: We've managed to catch a few more, either by gunpoint or in mines [mine fields].

Krstić: Kill them all, God damn it!

Obrenović: Everything is going according to plan.

Krstić: Single one must not be left alive.

Obrenović: Everything is going according to plan. Everything.

Krstić: Way to go, chief. The Turks are probably listening to us. Let them listen, the motherfuckers. [Turks is a derogatory name for Muslims in Bosnia.]

There was a short pause after the prosecutor had played the tape. He looked at Krstić. Everybody looked at him. General Krstić lowered his head and covered his face with his hands. It was a gesture of sheer despair. As though he might burst into tears. It must have been clear to him that this was the end of everything – of his hope of finishing his trial with his integrity and his officer's honour intact. This was the end, and he knew it. He was devastated. Sitting in the courtroom in the dock, he seemed to have shrunk, seemed suddenly more vulnerable than ever. Once again, I felt pity for him, because he had miscalculated so badly. He had apparently not counted upon the prosecution having such damning evidence as that taped conversation.

'General Krstić, did you, on 2 August 1995, tell Major Obrenović to kill the people he captured that day?' the prosecutor asked him. Suddenly, in a dramatic transformation, Krstić almost shouted at him: 'No, Mr McCloskey! This is one hundred per cent montage! On that day I didn't talk to Obrenović at all. Second, I did not recognise the other participant in the conversation, and especially not my own voice, myself. I repeat: This is a montage, one hundred per cent rigged.'

It was the only moment during the entire trial that Krstić reacted strongly, almost militantly. It was probably because he was truly scared that he had been caught lying and his actions had finally caught up with him. After all, Krstić had given the order to kill. He had actually said those words, even if he denied it.

Yet, although the taped conversation had been intercepted by two different sources, the court refrained from taking it into consideration when the judges decided upon his sentence; they had enough other evidence.

After Srebrenica, Krstić had apparently signed a document in support of General Mladić in his power struggle with the President Radovan Karadžić. At that time, Krstić – as he himself admitted – was aware that Mladić had committed war atrocities. 'I had to sign it because all the other generals signed it – can you imagine what would have happened to me if I had not signed it?' he said, his tired voice quavering slightly. It was the end of the day. McCloskey looked at Krstić; by now even he appeared to feel sorry for him. Then he listed the names of five generals who had not signed the document and were still alive and well. He asked Krstić the question that every single person in that courtroom probably wanted to ask him: 'Why didn't you just retire, General, when all this happened? Was that the right choice, General? Did you make the right choice?' It was the *coup de grâce*. General Krstić, crushed and demoralised, could only reply, 'I'd rather not answer that question.'

Perhaps Krstić was naive enough to believe that, if he had only been skilful enough, he could have tricked the prosecution, convinced them that Mladić was the only culprit. Krstić wanted to portray himself as a bystander, but in war there are no bystanders. In Srebrenica, General Krstić was most definitely not one. He was heavily implicated. Or, in the words of Judge Almiro Rodrigues: 'But you were there, General Krstić, you heard, you gave orders, you knew! You were there when they began to separate the men from the women, children and old people. You could not *not* have seen their physical condition. You could not *not* have heard the screams of the men who were taken to the building called the White House as they were being beaten.'

The man who had entered the courtroom with an air of naiveté, compliant and ready to please the judges, but who did not have the guts to confront Mladić – who portrayed himself as a victim of circumstances – this man was at last utterly revealed. In his trial was the evidence of the collapse of a society that had lost its values, of an army that had lost its honourable reputation and of the man who had lost his soul when he 'agreed to evil'.

8

One Day in the Life
of Dražen Erdemović

Dražen Erdemović, born in 1971 in Tuzla, Bosnia, of a Croatian mother and a Serbian father, was accused of crimes against humanity for taking part in a massacre of Muslim men from Srebrenica on 16 July 1995. During the investigation and the trial, he repeatedly expressed his remorse for the crimes he had committed. Erdemović explained that he had been forced to shoot because, when he refused, his commander had threatened him with death. His initial sentence was ten years in prison, but on appeal it was reduced to five years, because the Tribunal acknowledged that Erdemović had acted under extreme duress. He was a witness for the prosecution in the Krstić case, as well as in the Karadžić–Mladić case. Today he is free and enjoys the status of a protected witness.

It was already past nine o'clock in the morning when Dražen Erdemović and his unit arrived at the Branjevo collective farm.

They had not been told what their task would be. Their commander, Brano Gojković, had not been very talkative during the bus ride from their base in Vlasenica; he hadn't even told his soldiers where they were going. Dražen did not like it. Their 10th Sabotage Detachment of the armed forces of Republika Srpska usually had clear tasks, like reconnaissance missions or planting explosives in enemy territory, and they were always informed about them well in advance. But this was different. Whatever the mission was, it was secret. The only thing Dražen knew was that they were bringing a lot of ammunition with them, for both pistols and automatic weapons.

It was not a long drive, and when they got out of the bus they found themselves near a farm. It was a pig farm, but it seemed deserted; there were no animals to be seen and no people except a lone watchman. There was a big oak tree in the yard, and Dražen and several other soldiers sat under it. Although it was still early in the morning, it was already hot. Dražen looked at the fields surrounding the farm, the nearby woods shimmering in the heat and the blue mountains beyond. The view was beautiful. It reminded him of the small village where his parents lived and where he used to spend his summers as a child. Bosnia was beautiful; he had always thought so. Not that he had travelled enough to be able to make comparisons, but he had heard this from others as well. If only he could go to a river and swim! Yes, that was what he wanted to do. Just as he had when he was a small boy, swimming in the stream near his village with his pals, feasting on a tomato and a piece of bread spread with lard that his grandmother had given him for lunch. Dražen could still remember the feeling when, hot from running, he would jump into the cold water, and then, afterwards, bite into a tomato warmed by the sun.

But he had not come to Branjevo to swim. He lit a cigarette, somewhat uneasy. What are we waiting for? he asked Ivan, a soldier sitting next to him, a Croat. But Ivan was not in a good mood either. Don't ask too much, he murmured. Dražen decided to let it go and lay down. The grass under the tree was still cool and wet from the morning dew. The sky above was so blue that it almost hurt his eyes. He closed them and let his thoughts drift. If only he could get out of the whole thing, the war, this uniform of his, the shooting. He had never liked being a soldier and never thought he was a good one. He had never demonstrated any enthusiasm for it and for this reason had not made much of a career in the army. Once he had been promoted, but he held his new rank for only two months before his superiors detected how reluctant a soldier he was. Things never worked out for him; it was almost as if there was an outside force determining his life. He should have stayed in Tuzla, but there was no work there for a locksmith, his occupation before he joined the army. Besides, all the men his age had been drafted into the Serbian, Croatian or Bosnian units. He was drafted by the Yugoslav National Army (JNA) in 1990, served as an army policeman in Belgrade, then was sent to fight the Croats in Slavonia. He came back to Tuzla in 1992 but was soon mobilised by the Croatian Defence Council (HVO) units in Herzegovina. After a year he got out of the HVO and for some time tried to avoid the war. Then he got married. Soon a baby was born. Things just seemed to happen to him. Like now. He was supposed to be in Switzerland, instead of this Branjevo. He and his wife had come to Republika Srpska because he had managed to arrange to get documents, so that they could leave their country gone mad. But when they arrived in Bijeljina, the man with their documents never showed up! So they were stuck there, with a baby boy and no money. Dražen had to find a job. Three months earlier a friend had told him that armed forces of Republika Srpska paid well and would provide him with a house, too. Indeed, Dražen was soon allotted a house that had belonged to a Muslim, but he considered being a soldier a temporary solution. He was much more concerned with trying to obtain the valid documents which would enable him and his young family to leave. This was the easiest way out – or so Dražen thought. But instead of going to Switzerland, he had ended up in Branjevo.

At first it was all right; his squad wasn't really involved in actual fighting. He had been a soldier for four years now, in different units and in different parts of what used to be Yugoslavia, but he was still finding this war unreal, just as when you are part of something but feel as if you're not really there. That was how Dražen felt: he was there, but never fully present in his uniform.

Lying in the grass now in the Branjevo farm, he felt the ground vibrating slightly. It reminded him of the time he had put his ear on a railway line and could hear the train coming long before it appeared from behind a nearby hill. He stood up and looked around. The others were not alerted yet, but they soon would be. A bus was coming towards them. It was a rather battered vehicle, one of those buses that take peasants between villages and breaks down more often than not. Dražen could see the name 'Centrotrans' on it in big letters and a few soldiers sitting in the front. It stopped before the main building, some fifteen metres from them. Their commander spoke briefly to the driver while two other soldiers opened the rear door. A man appeared. Dražen will remember him forever, because at that moment it became clear to him what their task was to be, and he suddenly shivered. The man was tall and very thin. He had a moustache, but Dražen could not tell his age because the man was blindfolded with a piece of dirty cloth. He wore a bluish shirt soaked with sweat, a pair of blue trousers with white stripes down the side and sneakers. His hands were tied behind his back. The man got down from the bus and took a few unsteady steps. More men followed; they were also blindfolded. A soldier marched them to a field alongside the farm.

The commander assembled his unit and told them that buses would be brought in carrying civilians from Srebrenica. He meant captured Muslim men who had surrendered to the units of Republika Srpska. They are to be executed by our unit, the commander told them. Dražen and his comrades-in-arms suddenly learned that their squad was to become a firing squad, and he didn't like it at all. Never before had they been assigned such a task. But nobody said a word. Only one of them, Pero, seemed eager to begin, but Dražen noticed that he was drinking from a bottle of brandy. Dražen looked at the prisoners. They were standing with their backs to the soldiers. One man half turned his head towards them, as if he expected something. Was there something he wanted from them? Dražen felt a strong revulsion and he was afraid that he would vomit.

No, he would not do it! He couldn't kill men just like that, point-blank. As he went up to his commander, his hands were trembling. I don't want to do this, he said. Brano Gojković turned towards Dražen, as if he had not heard him properly. What? he said. Dražen knew the trick. Gojković wanted him to repeat his words loud enough for everybody to hear, so that he would have witnesses for whatever might happen next. Dražen looked at the soldiers. Comrades, I don't want to do this. Are you normal? Do you know what you are doing? he said, but less firmly, feeling his bravery quickly evaporating as the others studiously avoided his eyes. Pero openly laughed at him. A moment of awkward silence followed. It occurred to

Dražen that he had not heard a single bird singing that day. Gojković looked at Dražen without flinching. His expression was serious. Erdemović, he said, if you don't want to do it, walk over there and stand together with the prisoners so that we can shoot you, too. Give me your machine gun!

Dražen must have understood instantly that the officer meant what he was saying. But he was confused; he had not expected such a reaction. He had hoped, briefly, that he could get out of this mess if he just said no. What did he expect? He remembered hearing about an earlier case of disobedience, when a soldier had been executed at the order of Lieutenant Colonel Pelemiš, and he realised that now it was too late to say no. He should have said it long ago. His heart was beating so strongly that he could hear nothing but its pumping. For perhaps a minute, or even less, Dražen just stood there with the Kalashnikov in his hands. For a moment he thought of running into the woods. But he saw the face of his wife before him, and he felt helpless. They could take revenge on her and the baby at any time. He was responsible for three lives. It was an excuse, yes; the truth was that he had proved to be a coward and he knew it, but what else could he have done? Gojković would not hesitate to order him killed and Pero would do it with pleasure, although Dražen did not understand what he had against him. Maybe the fact that Dražen was not a pure Serb, which made it even more advisable to take Gojković's threat seriously.

The commander was no longer looking at him, as if he had no interest in his decision. He ordered the soldiers to take up a position behind the prisoners and the prisoners to kneel on the ground. Dražen took his place at the end of the squad. His heart was still beating loudly when he aimed at an elderly man whose face, luckily enough, he had not seen before. He quickly, feverishly, weighed up his options. Of course, he

could fire between two prisoners. But his prisoner would still
have to be killed. Like having to die twice. Besides, their firing
squad was a small one of only a dozen soldiers, and if he didn't
aim properly it could be detected immediately. The
commander would know, and he would be executed. No, he
must aim properly. Then a command came – 'Shoot!' – and the
man disappeared from his view. He remembered only that his
first victim wore a grey T-shirt. Dražen closed his eyes and
tried to calm himself down. But the new prisoners were
already in front of him. One of them shouted: Fuck you,
bloody . . . and did not even have time to finish his sentence
before the command to fire came again. Once he started,
Dražen kept shooting every few minutes without thinking
much about what he was doing. The only thing he was aware
of was trying to aim at elderly people rather than young ones –
it seemed less of a waste. Soon the bus had been emptied.

When Dražen looked at his watch, he was shocked: it had
taken them only fifteen minutes to execute some sixty people!
A second bus had already arrived. The men in the bus could
not see what was awaiting them as they were blindfolded, too.
Dražen was glad about that; he thought this was actually an
act of mercy towards these poor men. But pretty soon after
that, buses began to arrive carrying men who were not
blindfolded. Their hands were not even tied. It was as though
they had been hurriedly pushed into buses and sent to the
Branjevo farm. But why such hurry? Dražen did not
understand. And there was something else that he did not
understand, that did not seem logical to him: these men who
came later could surely see what was about to happen to them.
They could see dead bodies on the ground and soldiers
standing there with Kalashnikovs. And yet, they stepped down
from the bus and marched to the execution site with two
soldiers. Why didn't any of them try to escape into the nearby

wood? Dražen wondered. In a couple of minutes you could dive into the safety of the trees; there was at least a slim chance of survival. But not a single prisoner tried to break away. Dražen had never seen such a spectacle before: prisoners walking in orderly fashion towards their execution site, like animals in a slaughterhouse. Did they believe somebody would save them? If all of them had tried to run, surely some would have reached safety. At the very least, they would die knowing that they had tried. They had nothing to lose. They were to be executed, and they must have known it the moment they got off the bus. Dražen wished they would try to run; at least it would give him a reason to shoot at them, and it would be more fair, because they would have had a chance to escape. But no. The prisoners were pouring in in a steady, peaceful stream as if some kind of mental paralysis had seized them.

Maybe these men no longer felt anything? But then he saw something and realised this couldn't be so. As he aimed at the nape of a man's neck, Dražen saw a telltale stain on the back of his trousers. There was a wet spot there, getting bigger and bigger. He heard a command and shot once more. When the man fell down, Dražen saw that he was still alive, still urinating out of fear. Dražen was suddenly embarrassed, as if it was happening to him. It could happen to me, too, he thought, but pushed the unpleasant notion away. He was tired and angry with himself, with Gojković, with everybody. It was just not right to execute all these men. If they were soldiers then they were prisoners of war, and if they were civilians, what was happening to them was even more unjustified. He and his fellow soldiers were doing something wrong, that much he knew. If there were any justice, then these men would not be executed just like that, without a trial, without any proof of their guilt. Hundreds of men could not disappear just like that. Their relatives would be looking for them, and eventually Dražen's unit would be held accountable for their deaths. If Gojković didn't want witnesses, what about his own soldiers? Were they not witnesses to the crime? How could he be sure that nobody would talk?

Just then, Dražen heard another noise. Among the prisoners standing in the field was a man of perhaps sixty, grey-haired and neatly dressed. Don't kill me, he shouted, I saved the lives of many Serbs in Srebrenica. I could give you their names, I am sure they would vouch for me. He started to pull a piece of paper out of his pocket. Dražen approached him and took him aside. He gave him a cigarette and a glass of orange juice. The man sat down and lit the cigarette. His hands were trembling as he handed the paper to Dražen. Here are names and telephone numbers, you can check them if you want, it's true what I am saying . . . But Dražen knew that the man would not be allowed to live, because he was already a witness to the execution. Why did he take him aside, then? Dražen was impressed by this man who had not silently accepted death like the others. He seemed honest and brave, and Dražen wanted to prolong his life for as long as he could. But the man did not look as if he had any hope left. We all used to live together, Muslims, Serbs, Croats, the man said to Dražen. What happened to us ordinary people? Why did we let it happen? Yes, indeed, what happened to us, Dražen said; if only somebody could explain that to me, if only I knew, but I don't know any more than you do, I am a half-Croat, my wife is a Serb.

Dražen understood that he and the man in front of him had something in common: they had nothing against people of other nationalities. But how could you do this? the man asked as he inhaled the smoke from the cigarette, sensing it would be his last. What could Dražen tell him but that he did not have a choice? It sounded like a stupid thing to say to a man about to lose his life, it sounded damned stupid. But it was the truth. Dražen was aware that the man was guilty only of being the wrong nationality, and in this he didn't have a choice either.

There was no more time for a conversation. Pero and another soldier approached them and took the man away. Dražen said no, don't do it, knowing that it was all he could do. Shut up, don't be stupid, Ivan said. In a minute it was over; the man was dead.

It must have been past noon, but the soldiers did not have much time for a break. At the beginning, every half-hour Dražen would go and sit under the tree and have a cigarette. It was a kind of escape, a break. But then he no longer craved a cigarette. His movements became more and more mechanical. He would aim at somebody's head and shoot, and before he had time to wipe his forehead the next one would be kneeling in front of him. He preferred it that way; if he paused for too long, he would become aware of the foul odour of the bodies. In the heat bodies started to decompose almost immediately. The stench reminded him of a butcher's shop. Sometimes his mother would send him to buy meat, though he tried to avoid it. In summer the stench in the butcher's shop was unbearable, and fat, green flies would land on pieces of raw meat to eat and lay their eggs. The butcher would entertain himself by catching flies and dropping them in a glass of water. Dražen would run home, eager to get away from the smell. What a fine nose you have, his mother would tease him. Now the same kind of stench was coming from the field, the same kind of green flies descending on the fresh bodies.

Ivan, perhaps noticing that Dražen was becoming nauseated, offered him a brandy, a strong homemade *šljivovica*. Dražen took several sips and felt better. With the alcohol taking over, he could keep shooting for some time without giving himself a chance to think. As he took another long sip of the *šljivovica*, Dražen saw out of the corner of his eye a young boy stepping down from a bus. The boy was not blindfolded and Dražen saw his face, though he had promised himself that he would not look at the prisoners' faces, as it made shooting more difficult. The boy might have been fifteen, perhaps younger. His chest was bare and his pale skin exposed to the sun. The boy looked at the soldiers and then at the rows of dead bodies in the field. His eyes grew bigger and bigger, as if he could not take in all that he saw. But he is a boy, only a boy, Dražen murmured more or less to himself, careful not to stand behind him. When the prisoners knelt down in front of the squad, just before the command to shoot came, Dražen heard the boy's voice. Mother, he whispered, Mother! That day Dražen heard men begging for their lives, grown men crying like children; he heard them promising money, cars, even houses to the soldiers. Many were cursing, some of them were sobbing. But this boy was just calling for his mother, as children sometimes do when they awake from a bad dream and all they long for is their mother's hand on their forehead. A minute later the boy was dead, but Dražen was sure he could still hear his voice. I am beginning to hallucinate, he thought. For the second time that day he felt so nauseous that he had to run to the bushes and vomit. Nothing came out except yellowish liquid smelling of alcohol.

The next bus had not yet arrived. Dražen leant against a tree, exhausted. It was already two o'clock. Since ten that morning he had been shooting, trying not to look at the prisoners, trying not to think about them, trying not to feel anything. Now he felt numb, his body as stiff as wood. He felt like a puppet on a string, able only to raise his hands and fire his gun again and again. He sat there staring at the horizon. He heard somebody wailing, then a solitary shot. Dražen did not turn his head; he did not want to see anything more, he had had enough of killing. How many more buses would come? After three o'clock in the afternoon it was over. Gojković announced that there would be no more arrivals, and they quickly boarded their own bus.

The sun was still high in the sky, and the stench in the air was unbearable. Dražen had to get away from this nightmarish place. Again, he wanted to jump into water or at least to take a shower and wash away the smell of death. If only he could wash his hands! Dražen carefully examined them. There was no blood on them, only a blister on his right index finger. A round, pink blister. How strange, Dražen thought, to get a blister from killing people. He estimated that he must have fired some seventy times. He had killed perhaps seventy people and got a blister! Suddenly, it was so funny that Dražen began to laugh hysterically.

At last they were leaving the Branjevo farm. The field was covered with corpses. Who would bury them? And where? Dražen turned his head away. This was no longer any of his business. He had done his part; for him it was over. For the first time that day he could breathe deeply.

But it was not over. Not yet.

When they arrived in neighbouring Pilice, the commander informed them that there were five hundred men in the House of Culture and that they also were to be executed. This time it was easier to say no, because Dražen was not the only one to do so. They were all tired from the killing and they refused to go on. But there were fresh soldiers who volunteered for the task and the commander accepted them. Dražen sat in a café across from the House of Culture and ordered a strong black coffee. Just before their group arrived, some Muslim men, prisoners from the House, had broken out and had all been killed as they ran down the street. Soldiers were still searching the corpses for money and gold. Dražen stared at them, just stared, sipping his coffee. It was too sweet.

Dražen knew that he would never forget this day, and that it would remain his curse: that smell of fresh air in the morning, the blue of the sky, the sound of the first bus arriving, the thin man with a moustache, another man's trousers soaked with urine, the stench of rotten meat, the dark red colour of blood gushing from a wound, the man who asked him how he could do what he was doing, the boy calling for his mother. He sensed that this day would change his entire life – that it was already changing. He felt tears coming. Boys don't cry, his father used to tell him when he came home with bleeding cuts on his knees. But where was his father now? Where were they all now – his parents, his wife, his friends? Dražen had never felt so alone, alone with twelve hundred dead bodies that would be with him wherever he went.

9

A Beast in a Cage

The case of Slobodan Milošević, the former President of Serbia and Yugoslavia, is the first international prosecution of a former head of state for crimes committed while in office. He is charged, among other things, with committing genocide during the war in Bosnia, as well as with crimes against humanity during the wars in Croatia and Kosovo. Although he most certainly did not kill anybody himself, he is responsible for the politics that resulted in the deaths of more than two hundred thousand people. Milošević has chosen to defend himself at the Tribunal.

Only a glass wall divided me from Slobodan Milošević in the courtroom in The Hague. He sat about six or seven metres away between two tall UN policemen – close enough for me to be able to study the expressions on his face, his body language and even the details of his clothing. He was dressed in a dark blue blazer, a pale blue shirt and a red, white and blue tie – the colours of the Serbian flag. His hair was completely grey, almost white. His skin was pale, the colour of dough, and he looked unhealthy, as though he had not seen the sun for some time.

Looking at him, I realised that I was surprised. I cannot say that I felt triumphant, as I had expected I would feel when I finally saw him in the dock. True, I was relieved to see him there, but nevertheless I felt very confused. This bothered me; it even made me angry. I had the privilege of observing the trial of the 'Butcher of the Balkans', the very symbol of evil in my lifetime, the man who set my country on fire – and yet, it was strange to see him in the courtroom.

It made me feel uncomfortable.

I quickly realised what was disturbing me. I had never actually dared to picture him in a courtroom. Even when he was proclaimed a war criminal, it was hard to imagine that one day he would actually be facing his judges in The Hague. When, on 5 October 2000, Milošević's party lost the election and he was arrested soon after, there was much talk about extradition. However, the new Serbian President vehemently rejected the very idea of it. Then, three months later, the new government, pressed by the need for money, delivered Milošević just like that. His price was exactly 1.3 billion dollars. He was flown to The Hague. It had finally happened.

But why couldn't I imagine such a development? Why didn't I think of it at all? Now it seems to me that I did not believe in the rule of law. Or that reinforcement of the law would be possible in Serbia, especially not in Milošević's case. After all, during the decade that he had been the President of both Serbia and Yugoslavia, he had behaved as if he himself was the law.

I remember – how could I ever forget it? – hearing the news on the radio in my kitchen in Vienna, on the morning of 1 April 2001. I was preparing my first espresso coffee of the day with the radio playing in the background, as usual. The news came on; there was something about Milošević. I turned the volume up. I was expecting news about him because he had been surrounded by the police in his Dedinje residence, and some sort of resolution was expected at any moment. In violent post-war Serbia (and considering his own family history), anything seemed possible: he might shoot at the police, the police might shoot at him, or he might commit suicide. 'Slobodan Milošević surrendered to the police last night, and he is in Belgrade's Central Prison now,' a male voice said on the radio. Surrendered? I stood in my kitchen, incredulous. Was it really true? How was it possible? That morning, the coffee was forgotten.

Almost three months later, on 26 June, I watched Christiane Amanpour on CNN in front of the prison in Scheveningen reporting that Milošević was about to land there. I stared at the TV as if I had just seen a ghost. Although this possibility had been discussed widely in the world press, I was still not prepared for it. And now here I was, in the courtroom, facing him, seeing him with my very own eyes, again bewildered, again angry with myself because of it. There was something about seeing this man sitting in the courtroom that was incongruous with my memories, with some hidden part of me. Of course I was glad that he was on trial. I was pleased that he would finally have to face justice. But it wasn't that simple. I realised, looking at him, that I was facing the personality cult I had grown up with. I was facing my life in communist Yugoslavia when I least expected it.

Suddenly I remembered a moment from my childhood. We were living in a small town on the Adriatic. It was May 1954 and it was a holiday. It must have been 1 May or perhaps 25 May, Tito's birthday, the 'Day of Youth'. My father and I were decorating our window. The window frame had a nail on which to hang Tito's framed portrait. The photograph we had seemed huge to me, although it was probably about thirty by forty centimetres and may even have been smaller than that, as I myself was very small. The portrait showed Tito in the snow-white uniform of a marshal. Or was it the uniform of an admiral? In those days there was no colour photography, at least not in Yugoslavia, so photographs were coloured by hand. In his desire to make Tito more handsome, the photographer had got carried away with his brush. Tito's eyes were too blue, his cheeks too rosy and his lips too red. When the picture was hung I handed my father several branches of ivy. He laid them loosely under the photograph, on two other nails at either end of the window frame. A few red carnations placed here and there, and the decorating was finished. We went into the street to look at it from the outside. Beautiful, isn't it? my father asked me. I nodded. Through the open window we could hear music from our radio. Cheerful marches added to my father's festive mood. I could smell the cake my mother was baking, and I liked our little ceremony even more.

I was only five and very proud to be allowed to help my father with such an important task. Our window was the only one in the entire apartment building decorated like this. It was because my father was an army officer, a commander of the local garrison. The picture of Tito surrounded by flowers reminded me of something that I had seen before, but I knew I was not supposed to mention it to my father. It was a secret. My grandma would sometimes take me with her to church. I usually felt a bit sick in the church because of the smell of white lilies, but I was fascinated by it. There I saw pictures and statues of Jesus, the Holy Mother and many saints, and they were all decorated with flowers, too. The decorated picture under our window was very similar to what I had seen in the church, and I thought that Tito, too, must have been a kind of saint in my father's church.

When I was at school, I participated eagerly in celebrating Tito by writing compositions about him, taking part in performances for his birthday, reciting poems about him and running in relay races in his honour. In our classroom the very same picture of Tito in his snow-white uniform hung above the blackboard, and we decorated it on every state holiday, just as we did at home. As a child, I thought it was normal to celebrate Tito in this way; everyone around me did it.

It was years before I learned that in Yugoslavia we were growing up with a personality cult. But what that really meant I saw only when Tito died in 1980. Tito himself did not quite understand that he was dying, as one of the doctors taking care of him in hospital in Ljubljana later told me. A leg had been amputated and his kidneys had failed, but Tito continued to talk about his plans for the future. Could it be that, once someone has ultimate power, he begins to believe in his own immortality as well? And others begin to believe in it too? After all, Tito had been in power for more than thirty years. It really looked as if he was going to be there forever.

It is easy to think that people in Yugoslavia would have been happy at last to get rid of a dictator – which Tito certainly was. But they were not happy. When he eventually died, they were surprised and devastated. I remember men and women crying in the streets for days after his death, wandering around like lost children. His death was a major catastrophe, like an earthquake or a flood. There was a feeling of terrible loss, of fear of what would happen next, a prevailing atmosphere of despair . . . It was easy for Slobodan Milošević to satisfy that emotional hunger. People were looking for somebody to take care of them. The orphaned nation needed a new father. When communism collapsed ten years later, people were even more lost, insecure and frightened, almost like young children forced to start living on their own. Besides, there were no other models of political leadership except for the authoritarian model of Tito.

Slobodan Milošević made his way to the top of the Communist Party structure, mercilessly ousting everybody in his way. But he was not a believer in communism. In 1987 he visited Kosovo Polje, the site of the battle of 1389 against the Turks, and delivered his ominous speech to the Kosovo Serbs, who are a minority among the Albanians there. His declaration 'No one shall ever beat you again!' quite unexpectedly launched him into the orbit of nationalist heroes. He began to incite Serbian nationalism with his speeches, but not because he wanted a war. He was not even a believer; he was not a messianic type of leader like the Croatian President, Franjo Tudjman. His speeches had no fire, no conviction. Most probably, what Milošević believed was that he could control the power of nationalism and manipulate it for his own benefit. He was a skilful demagogue riding on the patriotic feelings of others. The paradox of Milošević is that he was neither a communist nor a nationalist, but an opportunist capable of using any ideology that would help him to remain in power. Opportunism might be his most important characteristic. If nationalism would help him stay in power – so be it.

So, there he was now, in gaol, after thirteen years of being a demi-god himself.

I did not expect him to surrender to the police in Belgrade; nobody expected it. I thought there would be some kind of violent end, similar to what had happened to Elena and Nicolae Ceauşescu in Romania in December 1989: a court martial followed by a quick execution. I remember well the last speech of Nicolae Ceauşescu a few days before his execution. He stood on a balcony of the Communist Party headquarters in Bucharest, addressing a huge mass of people below in the city's main square. Suddenly he heard a strange sound, a sound he was not used to. Instead of applause, for the first time in his life he heard the noise of anger. Comrade Ceaușescu did not understand what was going on, one could see it in his face. He was totally surprised. His beloved Romanians! His children! How could they turn on him? I could imagine how Milošević must have felt during those last moments in his house in Belgrade, surrounded by his own police. Surely his people would come to defend him, their beloved leader. But they did not come. People let him down, as they have the habit of doing with dictators.

If Slobodan Milošević and his wife had met a brutal end like the Ceaușescus, it would have been fitting: a bloody regime ending in blood. Milošević's victims would have been vindicated, and his followers would have a martyr. Everybody would be pleased. If, on the other hand, he had committed suicide, that would have made sense too. Much had been written about his parents' suicide, and it was not unrealistic to expect that Milošević would follow suit. But for such a course of action a person has to be brave, has to have a sense of drama. His suicide could have been a grand departure from the world's stage, a romantic ending, a heroic way of telling the world that he had no intention of surrendering to his enemies. Milošević could have ensured his place in the memory of the Serbian people and become as beloved as Prince Lazar Hrebljanović from the epics about the battle against the Turks at Kosovo Polje. His death might have been a catharsis for the Serbian people, marking the end of authoritarianism.

But Milošević is a bureaucrat. He is simply too small, too ordinary for such dramatic gestures. One explanation why Serbs turned away from him so quickly following his imprisonment was that they were disappointed in him for just that reason – for allowing himself to be arrested. He was not the person they had believed him to be, the hero they had nicknamed 'Freedom' (Slobo-Slobodo). He was just an ordinary man, afraid for his life. Seeing him surrender like a petty thief must have been humiliating for everybody who had believed in him. They had worshipped him as if he were a god! And he was just one of them after all? His surrender made people look childish and foolish, and they were not going to forgive him for that.

Indeed, he really had been loved in Serbia: three times voted into office in democratic elections, twice as President of Yugoslavia and once as President of Serbia. He ruled like a monarch, as if there were no parliament, Prime Minister or democratic procedures of any kind. The only person he sought advice from was his wife, Mira Marković. People in Serbia used to say that their country had two rulers instead of one. As much as they loved him, they hated her, because of her influence on him, but she was protected by him. They were close to each other, to the exclusion of everybody else, almost as though they were an autistic couple whose love for each other carried them further and further away from reality.

Now Slobodan Milošević tried to make up for his failure – for his miserable surrender – with his behaviour in the courtroom.

At first, he made quite an impression: he faced the judges alone, without lawyers. He took care to look directly into the cameras, showing no fear or intimidation. He spoke fluently, although not in perfect English, which was his great advantage. Composed and focused, he projected the image of a brave individual caught up in an unjust battle. His very first statement to the Tribunal was, 'I don't recognise this court, this court is a false court and the indictments are false indictments.' He even won some sympathy from the public when Judge Richard May cut him short in the middle of his speech. After all, political speeches were his only interest. But the judge snapped at him, 'Mister Milošević, will you be quiet, please!' as if scolding a child. Later, Milošević seemed to be losing his nerve. He would shout abuse at the judges, like an angry adolescent.

He denied any wrongdoing on his part. Regarding the war in Bosnia, for example, alluding to the Dayton Agreement of 1995, he claimed that he had brought peace to Bosnia, not war. We had already seen how far his denial of reality had gone when he delivered a short speech on television after signing the capitulation following the NATO bombardment in 1999: Milošević congratulated the Serbs on winning the war. It was like George Orwell's novel *Nineteen Eighty-Four*: in Milošević's Serbia lies became truth, war became peace and defeat became victory.

From his very first appearance at the Tribunal, there was a kind of game going on in the courtroom between Milošević and the judges. Milošević would sit with his head turned away from the judges; he avoided looking at them, as if the whole thing had nothing to do with him. He appeared relaxed, disinterested in the long exchanges between the judges and the prosecution about the technical details of the proceedings. Instead, his eyes were scanning the members of the public, perhaps looking for familiar faces. At one point, something like a smile appeared on his face, which otherwise showed nothing but contempt. But his relaxed pose was no more than that: a pose. Like a hunted animal, he was wary of ambush. The moment he was given the word, he began to talk with great energy.

'Acting' is the word I would use to describe his behaviour in court. And for a bureaucrat, Milošević is a good actor. The atmosphere in the courtroom instantly changed every time he started to speak, as it was evident that he was determined to set the tone of the performance. Perhaps his most significant decision was not to hire a defence lawyer but to represent himself. But he was not going to defend himself; he was going to deliver political speeches. His wife, Mira Marković, said in an interview, 'As my husband does not consider himself guilty, he will not defend himself. He will only speak.' Apparently, this was a logical decision: you don't need a lawyer to deliver a political speech. A lawyer would not raise political issues. Milošević, on the other hand, was interested only in politics, not in law, not even in the legality or otherwise of the Tribunal *per se*, but in promoting his political aims. He would speak in court because it would allow him to air his own ideas. He could have chosen to defend himself through silence. However, his plan was not to save himself or to reduce his punishment.

Milošević's strategy was rather transparent from the very beginning: he was in court not to be tried, but to put others on trial. There was nothing spontaneous about his performance. It was planned, with two main objectives. First, he would make his trial look like a show trial. At one of the pre-trial hearings he told the judges that they might as well deliver their sentence in advance. Second, he would establish his own 'truth', which was that both he and his country were victims of a conspiracy. After all, he wanted to be remembered as a champion in defence of his country.

Once he got to say his piece for CNN and the other media, he would throw the 'truth' back in their faces. He told the whole world what he thought of the court. He explained that his was a political trial, of course – and that the court was an illegal and a political, not a judicial, institution. He explained that this was a plot by the most powerful countries to conquer a small, independent Balkan country. He told the world how hypocritical those Western leaders were, who only yesterday were making deals with him. Back then he wasn't a war criminal, but a 'factor of stability'. When he refused to obey their demands, when he did not want to bend to their wishes and become their slave, then his country was bombed and he was proclaimed a war criminal.

And so he did speak, time after time, on every possible occasion: as he saw it, he was fighting for freedom and independence and against international terrorism. He saw himself as a kind of Nelson Mandela, one could say, or like Tito himself. When Tito was put on trial in the former Kingdom of Yugoslavia for his illegal communist activities, he said, 'I only recognise the judgement of my own party.' By adopting Tito's attitude – you have got me, all right, I am your prisoner, but it doesn't mean that I will respect you or that I will obey your rules – Milošević was behaving like the leader of the then forbidden Communist Party in the thirties.

In The Hague, Milošević tried to do what Serbs had always been good at – presenting themselves as victims of historical events, of plots, of misunderstandings and the wrongdoings of others. And these court appearances gave him the chance to demonstrate his extraordinary ability to adapt to any new situation and then use it to his own advantage. The courtroom was an international stage, he realised, and, thanks to the media, he could play his role before the world. He knew a bit about the importance of the media. When he took power in 1987, he immediately got rid of all the chief editors of the important newspapers and the heads of the television and radio stations. From then on the media were strictly controlled – and became his main instrument for maintaining power for over a decade.

Milošević needs a public. He needs it at home, though he is probably not fully aware of how little support he enjoys now. He probably still believes he is addressing huge masses of his followers, although the majority of Serbs have already forgotten him. Also, as a dedicated politician, Milošević has borrowed James Bond's credo: 'Never say never again.' In the volatile political situation in Serbia, as well as in the world in general, he thinks he may yet have a chance to seize power again. The fact that he is in gaol doesn't distract him from his aims. That situation can change as quickly as it does in the James Bond movies.

But he needs the public abroad even more. As long as he is at the centre of attention, he has the opportunity to put forward his version of history, and this is his most important task during the trial in The Hague. He has to convince people that black is white, and he will only have a chance to do this if he has access to the media. His main endeavour now, as it has long been, is not to present events as they really happened, but to create history, just as he created reality earlier.

The more I watched him in the courtroom, day after day, and the more familiar I became with his gestures – his eyes scanning members of the public, his grimaces, his movements, his tics – the more I realised that I didn't know anything about this man. He was not only one of the biggest villains of the twentieth century, but he also changed my life. I cannot but wonder who Slobodan Milošević really is. What kind of person is hiding behind that aggressive attitude, that pale face, that stream of words? Who is the man behind the actor, behind the politician? Interestingly, I did not feel the need to know what was behind Tito's public face; what we saw was good enough for me. Milošević is a very private person, but that fits well the authoritarian model – both Tito and Stalin were secretive about their private lives as well.

Much has been written about Milošević, most of it about his political career and his role during the war. It is known that his parents killed themselves, that he met his wife very early, that he has two children and few friends, and that he cares very deeply only about his family. Not much beyond that is known, and certainly not enough for us to understand what makes him tick. It is almost as if this man has no persona other than his public one.

I read four biographies of Slobodan Milošević and the diary of his wife Mira Marković, all in the hope of understanding what motivated the man. But every new biography added to my disappointment. The books, by Dusko Doder, Florance Hartmann, Slavoljub Djukić and Vidosav Stefanović, all focus on just one or two aspects of him: his climb to the presidency and his role in the war. They are political biographies. Nonetheless, from time to time there emerges from the writing a shrewd, merciless, unsentimental Communist Party bureaucrat who is, above all, an opportunist.

But what I missed in these biographies of Milošević was the other side of him, his private face. It seemed his biographers could only touch the surface, the shell but not the essence of the man. The four books provide no details about his behaviour behind the public scene, about his relations with other people, his collaborators, his friends, his wife or children – something that would give us an idea about who he really is.

We, the public, are convinced that people like him – important people, political leaders, even when they are villains – must be interesting in their private lives as well. We want to know why they act as they do, and we believe we might discover their motives and reasoning in their biographies. But when one experienced journalist after another seems unable to reveal another dimension of Milošević, it makes me wonder: what if there is nothing to write about?

What is most revealing about Milošević's personality are perhaps his own words. In the spring of 2002 the Croatian weekly *Globus* published a series of transcripts of his conversations taped by the Croatian secret police between 1995 and 1998. The conversations took place in the Karadjordjevo hunting lodge, a luxurious residence just outside Belgrade where Tito used to wine and dine his foreign guests, and they include exchanges with the President of Serbia, Milan Milutinović, with Milošević's brother Bora (the Serbian ambassador in Russia) and with members of his own family. There are two striking things about the conversations. First, Milošević, by then President of Yugoslavia, gives direct orders to Milutinović and calls the chief editor of *Politika* (the leading Serbian daily) to tell him what to write about and how to write it. The other astonishing thing is the vulgarity of his language. Milošević's every second word is 'fuck', as if he were incapable of expressing himself in any other way.

Conversations with his wife and his children take up the greatest part of the transcripts. Though the family is close, Marija and Marko grew up as typical children of powerful parents. Marko became famous for his connections with gangsters and murky business deals that made him rich, and Marija for her liking of guns and gangsters and her habit of picking her lovers from among her bodyguards.

Milošević calls his wife 'baby', and she calls him 'beauty'. He tells his son, who wants to have plastic surgery, that he is 'as beautiful as his father'; he expresses irritation at his daughter's latest boyfriend. But more telling, it seems to me, is the fact that the transcripts actually portray the same picture of Slobodan Milošević as his four biographers do. There is nothing interesting about him as a private person, full stop. The transcripts, like the biographies, reveal all there is to know about this man: his banality, vulgarity and emptiness. There is no elegance or grandeur about him, not a single interesting thought, nothing to inspire curiosity. All in all, Milošević appears to be just a boring character surrounded by corrupt children and a wife thirsty for power. In history, he may have played a gigantic role, the role of a villain, but he appears to be a dwarf. A small, angry, autistic man. Deserted by his followers, now behind bars.

What illustrates his character best, perhaps, is an episode from the court. At the end of his cross-examination of a prosecution witness, Nikola Samardžić, Milošević asked him if he was familiar with the Serbian proverb 'People who lie have short legs.' The judges and onlookers were astonished. An awkward silence fell on the courtroom, as if no one could quite believe what Milošević had just said. Everybody present, including Milošević, knew that the witness, Samardžić, indeed had short legs. Not because he was lying, but because he had had them amputated as a result of complications from diabetes. Day after day he entered the courtroom slowly, cautiously, with a help of a stick. But this meant nothing to Milošević. He could not restrain himself from making a cruel 'joke'. This was not because he had poor taste. The reason ran much deeper. To Milošević, another man's suffering means nothing. He can feel no empathy for others. And he made me understand for the first time a definition of evil that I read somewhere long ago: evil is absence of empathy.

When I saw him for the last time in the courtroom, it was evident that he was becoming increasingly agitated. He was furious. He moved back and forth in his seat. He took his jacket off. He pulled faces. He tried to speak but was silenced by the judge. He stopped speaking English and would speak only Serbian; perhaps he had grown too frustrated to keep taking the time to show off. At the beginning, he had made me feel like a child visiting the zoo. I was watching a once dangerous wild animal now in captivity, and I felt thrilled but also a little uneasy, awestruck but apprehensive, incredulous at being so close to the beast, almost close enough to touch it. Maybe Milošević did not realise it yet, but this was exactly what his situation had come to: that of a beast in a cage. This man who had not lifted a finger in violence, but who, because of his decade-long murderous nationalist politics that had thrown Yugoslavia into a whirlpool of death and chaos, was responsible for the deaths of more than two hundred thousand people.

10

Ribbons and Bows

Mirjana Mira Marković is the wife of the longtime
President of Serbia, Slobodan Milošević. A professor of
sociology at the University of Belgrade, for more than
a decade she was the most influential person in
Milošević's life, directly influencing his political
decisions and determining the destiny of many people.
Because of this, she was the most feared woman in
Serbia and earned the nickname 'Lady Macbeth'.
Although she considered herself an academic, a writer
and an intellectual, she also had political ambitions
and was the president of the JUL (Yugoslav United
Left) Party. In February 2003 she fled to Russia,
sought by the Serbian police because of her suspected
involvement in the death of Milošević's opponent Ivan
Stambolić, whose body was found on 28 March 2003.

Every time I see a photograph of Mira Marković, Slobodan
Milošević's wife, or her image on television, I feel the urge to
tell her that her hair and her dresses are so hopelessly

unfashionable that she really must do something about them. Not that I am myself a fashion slave. But she looks so far from stylish, or even tasteful. Perhaps she is not aware of how old-fashioned she looks, or perhaps she doesn't care. But I can't help wondering why she chooses to dye her hair so black and wear it in a style that looks more like a helmet or a wig than a hairdo? The severity only hardens her face and makes her wrinkles look deeper. She could read in any women's magazine that strong, dark colours make you look older, and that the older a woman becomes the lighter she should colour her hair. But perhaps, as an intellectual and a feminist, Mira Marković doesn't read such superficial magazines? That's too bad; it might put her in tune with her times.

I can only assume that she would like to look younger, just as the rest of us would. If this were the case, she would certainly wear her hair in some other style, not with a fringe. Fringes are for girls and young women. We wore them in the late fifties and early sixties. At that time, there was only one film magazine, *Filmski svijet* (*The World of Film*), and that was our window to the world of fashion and glamour. We collected pictures of film stars, exchanged them and stuck them into albums. Many film stars of that time had fringes, like Brigitte Bardot and Audrey Hepburn. But the most striking fringe of all was worn by Elizabeth Taylor in her role as Cleopatra. Perhaps Mira saw the hairstyle years ago in the cinema in Požarevac, or she, too, read *Filmski svijet*, and the fringe impressed her so strongly that she was never able to stop wearing them. Nowadays, her hair still makes her look like Cleopatra, except she is no Elizabeth Taylor.

Where else could young Mira get ideas on how to do her hair or how to dress? In the fifties and sixties only a few people in my country had a television set at home. The programmes were in black and white – we couldn't get colour

TV for many years after it was invented – and in Yugoslavia one could see only foreign shows. Our neighbours had a television set and when they watched it, usually on Saturdays, the whole neighbourhood would congregate in their living room to watch. Italian TV shows were very spectacular, with elegant hosts and hostesses and dancing girls dressed in beautiful, glittering dresses. We girls – and our mothers – were flabbergasted by all that glitz, and we got all kinds of ideas about fashion and beauty from TV. If we saw a dress we wanted, we would have to describe it to a seamstress or run it up ourselves. My mother was very good at that, at turning coats inside-out or making children's clothes from grown-ups' clothes. But she was also capable of making a fine evening dress from an ordinary piece of material. Although there were no fashion boutiques at the time, thanks to her skill and imagination she was always well dressed.

There was, of course, a place women could shop, called NAMA, or People's Store, the very first chain of department stores in Yugoslavia. I remember the one in Rijeka. My mother did not buy her clothes there, but I loved visiting it because it was the biggest store in town and there were all kinds of interesting things to see there. What fascinated me most of all were the mannequins of women and men and even children in the shop window. I suppose they were made of plaster, with painted eyes and mouths and painted hair as well – kind of weird sculptures. There they stood, stiff and motionless, dressed in clothes that hung sadly on them fixed with pins behind their backs.

When I look at Mira Marković, I can't help but think of standing in front of the old NAMA shop window. Except for the fact that she is plump rather than thin, she looks like a mannequin who has just stepped out of the window display wearing a shapeless little two-piece 'set' in dark blue, or a huge blouse with a small, light print, made from cheap material and badly cut. As if the function of her clothes was just to hide her body. My spinster aunt would wear baggy clothes too (it's funny to think that she was considered a spinster at the age of thirty-eight). My aunt also wore orthopaedic shoes. My mother probably needed orthopaedic shoes herself because she had flat feet, but would never have dreamed of wearing them. She liked shoes with extremely high heels, like elegant sandals made of black patent leather. Good shoes were difficult to come by in the old Yugoslavia. Once or twice a year my mother would go to Trieste to buy them, and I would accompany her. Then she had to smuggle them back into the country. She never had any trouble, though: she would simply wear them through customs. It always worked.

I doubt Mira ever went to Trieste; it is too far from Požarevac. She was probably sentenced to wearing those terrible Borovo shoes – the kind of shoes worn by waitresses, hairdressers and other women whose jobs require them to be on their feet all day – until she became the First Lady. And by then perhaps she had become used to them.

Her whole style illustrates that she grew up in a communist country and is still used to the fashion that was created for post-war *drugarice* – that is, female comrades during communist times. This style was characterised by its distinct lack of femininity. It was as if women were advised to look more like men, or at least neutral. The message was that they could hold responsible jobs and positions only at the expense of their femininity, so women consciously played it down – that is, if they had any (and sometimes one really wondered about it). Maybe Mira Marković subconsciously adopted that 'comrade' style. Or perhaps she thought that if women were equal to men, they did not need to make an effort to look nice.

But I strongly doubt that this is the case with her. There is one thing about Mira that indicates that she is not only extremely feminine, but also quite coquettish. Mira Marković seems to like wearing some sort of decoration in her hair – a plastic flower, a ribbon, a bow – often brightly coloured, in contrast to her drab clothes. Such accessories have become her trademark. Her bows remind me of my childhood. As babies, all women of my generation were photographed wearing bows. When I was small there was a custom – which probably died out with my generation – of taking an 'official' photograph of a baby. The baby was usually about a year old when it was taken to the photographer, as very few people had their own cameras. It would be undressed and put on its stomach on a piece of cloth or a fur. The child would prop itself up with its hands and lift its head up, often displeased at finding itself in such an uncomfortable position. If it was a girl, the mother would tie a bow on to the baby's thin hair. Bows and ribbons were still fashionable in the late fifties, when Mira probably began wearing them. I was no exception: before going to school in the morning, my grandmother would comb my long hair into two plaits and decorate it with two big white bows like butterflies. Later, I wore ribbons in my hair, too, but that was in the sixties and the ribbons were just to hold my hair back.

Why would Mira Marković wear flowers, ribbons and bows as a teenager would? There is a story behind the plastic flower that she used to wear in the nineties. Mira was brought up by her maternal grandparents. Her mother was killed when Mira was only eight months old. All her life she was stigmatised because of her mother's terrible faith: it was said that her mother had denounced her Belgrade Communist Party colleagues while being tortured in prison by the Germans. Her father, a high Communist Party functionary and a war hero, did not acknowledge Mira until she was fifteen. They were never close, nor did she ever become friendly with her three half-sisters and her half-brother. Her mother's destiny greatly influenced young Mirjana, who took her mother's name, Mira, as her nickname. Not only could she not accept that her mother had committed treason, but she also took revenge on anyone who believed it was true, even on her own father. Mira idealised her mother as a pure and committed communist. Once she came across a photograph of her wearing a flower in her hair. Since that, in memory of her, Mira often wore a plastic flower in her hair, too.

But why a bow? Today the bow in Mira's hair looks totally incongruous with her matronly appearance. In fact, it looks grotesque. Could it really be only a matter of bad taste? Why would she want to look like this?

But the moment she starts to speak, everything falls into place. In a way, her voice explains her looks. One expects a deep, strong, almost masculine voice to match her coarse features, or at least the voice of a woman of a certain age. But her voice comes as a complete surprise and, for a moment, one wonders if it is genuine. She has a high-pitched, childish voice, the voice of a teenage girl. As well as this, she lisps like a child who never learned how to speak properly. And the more nervous she gets, the more obvious is her lisp.

As I look at her and listen to her voice – in an interview she is giving on television – I think of tone of those wooden Russian babushka dolls, one inside the other. To me, Mira is like that, one person within another. This extraordinary voice does not belong to the heavily built, middle-aged woman we see on the outside but to the little girl inside. That girl, in fact, is the real Mira, as she sees herself and, more importantly, as her husband sees her: not a sixty-year-old woman but a sixteen-year-old girl with bangs and ribbons. She wants to look and sound as she did when she and Slobodan Milošević first met and fell in love at high school in Požarevac in 1958. Under Mira's magic spell, time has stood still for both of them.

The fragile girl inside Mira needs protection. When she, with her girlish voice, turns to Slobodan, he is unable to resist. And if he tries to resist, she bursts into tears. Just like a little girl, she plays games with him, crying not because she is upset but to get her own way. This is part of her spoilt-girl repertoire, or at least this is what people who know them say about her. But Slobodan still seems to see her as she was at high school: a young, insecure, rather plain, lonely and helpless little girl. That is, until she met him.

Slobodan could understand her because he too came from a broken family. His father left him, his older brother and his mother, who was a teacher, and went to Montenegro. Slobodan grew up a lonely, serious boy without friends. He was a good pupil, one of those who sits in the front row of the classroom and listens attentively but does not participate in sports or other such activities. Slobodan and Mira met in December 1958, when she was sixteen and he was seventeen. From that time, Mira was no longer 'afraid of the dark, the cold or of getting poor marks for mathematics', as she wrote in one of her books.

Since then they have been inseparable. They became so devoted to each other, so absorbed with each other, that people in Požarevac used to call them Romeo and Juliet. To me, however, they are more like Hansel and Gretel: two little children deserted by their parents. As in the fairy tale, they have managed to save themselves. But they still live in the wild and threatening woods and perceive themselves as two abandoned orphans clinging to each other in order to survive. Tragedy in Slobodan's family brought them even closer together. When he was a student in his early twenties, his father committed suicide. Ten years later, his mother hanged herself. But Slobodan and Mira still had each other. They did not need other people. The world could no longer touch them.

Today, he probably sees in her the same vulnerability and helplessness and still rushes to protect her. But when I look at her, I see a shrewd, calculating, cold woman, not vulnerable at all and certainly not helpless. But this is beside the point, because neither of them cares a hoot about how other people see them. They only care about each other. In fact they go through life as if no one else exists. When we are young we often imagine that ideal love is when you find a soul mate, someone who almost becomes part of you. Someone you can trust completely, who will never let you down. Most of us soon realise that love isn't like this. Occasionally we see couples who seem to have just such a relationship. But there is usually something odd about them, as though they are encased in their own little cocoon, afraid to leave it. The longer they are together, the more alienated from the world they seem to become.

Mira and Slobodan are devoted to each other and to their children, and nobody outside their little autistic haven can touch or move them. Only Mira could turn this cold, calculating man into a caring and tender person. After about forty years together, they still call each other names like 'pussycat' and hold hands when they go for a walk. People close to them – although there are not many and they don't like to talk – swear that he has never been unfaithful to her. Once, allegedly, a secretary made a pass at Slobodan, who shouted at her, 'This is not a brothel!'

In his office Milošević displayed only one photograph, that of Mira. Indeed, it is not possible to write about him without taking into consideration his wife's influence – as it is not possible to write about her and her 'achievements' without mentioning the fact that she is married to Slobodan Milošević. They only function as a couple, as two parts of a whole. They derive power from each other, creating a relationship that excludes everybody else, and their behaviour eventually brought Milošević to where he is now – on trial in The Hague. He, a party apparatchik, was willing to pay any price to remain in power. She supported him unconditionally. When her Slobodan discovered nationalism as a means of remaining in power, she stood by him. When he became a populist dictator, she still stood by him. Her support was all that he needed.

Mira is the key to Slobodan Milošević: she is the one that makes him tick. She is the driving force behind him, the ambitious other half that pushed this rather colourless party bureaucrat to grasp every opportunity for power. As is sometimes the case with couples who have been married for a long time, they have also begun to look more and more alike. Small, dark eyes, thin lips, broad, coarse faces, and two deep lines running from their noses to the corners of their mouths, pulling their faces down with gravity. But they are still different in many ways. In photographs he never smiles, but she often does. She is communicative, he is reclusive; she is vain, he is not; she is ambitious, he is an opportunist; she cares about her image, he does not; she is an aspiring intellectual, he is a bureaucrat. However, the insatiable hunger for power is something they have in common.

Mira Marković was not satisfied with just being the First Lady. She wanted more. A reader could conclude that simply by studying the dust jacket of her book *Between East and South*, published in Belgrade in 1996. There she is described as a tenured professor on the Natural Science and Mathematics Faculty of Belgrade University, a member of the Russian Academy of Sciences, honorary professor of the Lomonosov University, director of the International Centre for Socio-political Research of Slavic Countries at the Russian Academy, and editor of two Russian–Yugoslav professional periodicals. Mirjana Marković is also the author of three sociology books and has published two volumes of her collected newspaper columns. Very much like Elena Ceauşescu, she never hid her ambition to become a prominent public figure and a leading intellectual. One of her cronies, a journalist from the daily newspaper *Politika*, in his desire to please Milošević has described her as 'one of the most important and interesting personalities of the scientific elite in the world'. In an autocratic society such as Serbia, honours and titles are not difficult to acquire, especially if you are the wife of the President.

But all this was not enough to satisfy Mira's ambition. She wanted to participate in politics directly, not merely through her husband, no matter how much influence that gave her. In 1994 she founded a political left-wing party called the JUL. This enabled her to operate in the same political arena as her husband. Soon the JUL had considerable influence in Serbian politics. Membership of her party was known to be a short cut to a good political position. Interestingly, Mira wanted to maintain a modest image and refused the position of president of the party, taking only the post of executive manager. But this did not fool anyone.

Mira always maintained a veneer of femininity and rarely demanded outright that her husband do this or that; rather, she seduced him into doing what she wanted. A man madly and blindly in love with his wife, eyewitnesses say it did not take much to persuade Milošević: a look, a gesture, the tone of her voice was enough. Moreover, he truly considers Mira to be a political and scientific genius. He was the most avid reader of her newspaper columns and willingly believed the critics who praised Mira's literary style and clever analysis.

It is hard to imagine that Mira would have risen to the position of an influential arbiter in Serbian society on her own merits as a Marxist professor of sociology. But the one who commands a powerful man is even more powerful than the man himself, as Mira wrote in one of her books: 'If a woman is capable of destroying the best man; if she – in spite of her average abilities – is capable of engaging better people than herself to turn her into a successful personality – then she deserves to enter a new century as his ruler.' Indeed, Serbia had not one ruler, but two. The fact is that Mira was able to use her position as the wife of a powerful man through the pathological hold she had on her besotted husband.

Mira Marković sees herself as a feminist. This is why she kept her family name. She often says that women are the stronger sex, but at the same time she likes to present herself as a romantic, delicate, sensitive soul with a special affinity for the arts: an aspiring writer and a lover of music. Full of contradictions, she is a Marxist and, until recently, was a member of the Communist Party – but she also believes in astrology. Her husband is proud of her independence and of her intellectual achievements. With his unreserved support, she began to believe she was important not only for him, but for the whole world as well.

In her book *Between East and South*, which is actually a diary she kept from 1994 to 1996, she gives her opinions on all kinds of subjects, ranging from garden flowers, wild birds, her children and the weather to an analysis of her political opponents. She often writes in a quasi-poetic style combining moralistic views and truisms: 'I always asked myself why birds return from the south when they fly there in the autumn. Is that because of a desire to fly to the north, or because of the hope that, for once, the autumn would not replace the summer there.' Her sentences contain sweeping, empty generalisations such as the following: 'The material and spiritual development is in a constant state of advance, an advance even faster as time goes by.' The only really interesting thing about this book is the fact that in it she hardly mentions the ongoing war in Bosnia. If she does say anything about war at all, it is to lament human nature: 'Above all the dead and wounded people one question hovers, the question without answer – why? Why are they dying, why are they disappearing, why have they lost their parents, children, friends, why are they wounded, why are they without houses and homeland, why do people behave more like animals than bloodthirsty animals themselves?' If I did not know who the author was, I would think these were the words of a naive teenager, not someone supposed to be able to make a political analysis. But written by Slobodan Milošević's wife, such words are sheer cynicism because she deliberately chooses not to acknowledge her husband's role in what she calls 'bloody orgies'. This was the time when Sarajevo was still under siege and snipers were daily killing people queuing for water or bread. In July 1995, the UN-protected enclave of Srebrenica fell and the soldiers of Republika Srpska executed some seven thousand Muslim men. But in her diary from this time, Mira Marković doesn't mention a word about any of it.

I imagine her sitting at her desk, looking out at her garden and writing about birds and clouds. After all, she did not see the dead or the refugees there. Nor, according to her own words, did she speak about them with her husband. Mira Marković was widely read in Serbia but not because of her eloquent style or her brilliant thoughts. Her column, published in a biweekly magazine called *Rainbow*, was read as a kind of political horoscope. It was common knowledge that if she criticised someone in her column, that person's career would soon be over. If Milošević disliked somebody and wanted to eliminate him politically, he would let Mira do the job. This was what happened to Mihajlo Marković. A well-known philosopher and a member of an international 'praxis' group of critics of Marxism (and no relation to Mira), he was the most prominent member and chief ideologist of Milošević's Socialist Party. But he supported Radovan Karadžić and Republika Srpska at a time when Milošević wanted to cut off all ties with them, so he had to be punished. The same happened to Borisav Jović, the former President of Yugoslavia, and Milorad Vučelić, head of Serbian television. Milošević stripped them of their party ranks in a seventeen-minute meeting with no further explanation. The explanations had already been given in one of his wife's columns.

It was not only people in politics who feared Mira. In Karadjordjevo, where Milošević and his wife were celebrating New Year's Eve in 1995, the electricity was cut off for several hours because of a technical problem. Mira wrote in her column that she believed it was an act of revenge arranged by political opponents who ruled Belgrade at the time. As a consequence, the entire managerial board of the electricity company was replaced overnight. A more tragic – to put it mildly – episode involved a journalist named Slavko Ćuruvija. He was a friend of Mira's until he had the audacity to tell her that Serbia, under the flag of the JUL and the Radical Party, was becoming a fascist country. Mira reacted vehemently in her column, calling him a traitor. A few months later he was murdered in broad daylight while walking down the street with his wife. Nobody could prove that Ćuruvija's murder had anything to do with Mira's condemnation of him. Perhaps people reading her columns were inspired to take justice into their own hands, but it seems more likely that it was a secret police operation. The secret police were adept at interpreting the unspoken and unconscious wishes of the Milošević–Marković family.

Likewise, anyone who was praised by Mira could expect promotion in the near future. Because of her arbitrary judgements and her profound influence over her husband, she was feared and hated even more than he was. She was Milošević's main, if not his only, political adviser. For a man who liked to decide everything single-handedly, as if state institutions did not exist, he depended heavily on her opinions. His biographers agree she had such a hold on her husband that some of his political opponents used to whisper that he ruled from under her petticoats. Therefore, although she was not indicted by the Tribunal in The Hague, she bears, at the very least, moral responsibility for his deeds.

Mira Marković was interviewed by Tim Sebastian on BBC TV in September 2001, not long after Milošević was extradited to The Hague. Hers was an extraordinary display. Dressed in a black skirt and blouse with white polka dots that could have come from my aunt's wardrobe, she sat stiffly in her chair, like a caricature of Cleopatra. Throughout the entire half-hour programme, she showed no emotion; the expression on her face never changed even when she was angry. The only things that moved were her pudgy hands, nails varnished bright red, her fingers adorned with huge rings. From time to time she touched her hair in a coquettish gesture.

Mira never actually answered a single question. Maybe she did not even listen to the questions. She must have agreed to the interview so that she could tell the world what she thought. She was not about to answer unpleasant questions put by some journalist. Tim Sebastian, for example, wanted to know why Slobodan Milošević, since his arrest, continued to insist that the Tribunal was illegal. 'Milošević did not object to the Tribunal when Radovan Karadžić and Ratko Mladić were indicted,' he pointed out. Mira retaliated viperously: 'Would you, please, behave as a journalist and an intellectual! You are interrogating me as if I were in a court! I did not accept the invitation to talk to you in order to feel uncomfortable but, as you said, in order that you could inform your public about an alternative opinion.'

As the interview went excruciatingly on, it became increasingly clear that Mira was someone who did not tolerate debate. She was deeply offended by Sebastian's questions and instead of answering she lectured him about the nineteen countries plotting against Yugoslavia and her heroic husband who 'fought for freedom and independence ... Our responsibility for that bloodshed is minor. The responsibility should be borne by those outside of Yugoslavia who financed this bloodshed.' When Sebastian asked her, very politely, the obvious question – did she believe that her husband would be released from prison in The Hague – she arrogantly brushed it aside: 'I don't want to answer that question! And don't look at me like that, I am not in a police station!' Confronted with such rudeness, Tim Sebastian, an experienced journalist who has interviewed all kinds of people, appeared completely at a loss.

As a professor, a party leader and First Lady, Mira Marković is not used to being questioned and certainly not to being contradicted. Her behaviour on the BBC echoed Milošević's performance in the courtroom. He will not listen to questions either, and when allowed to speak he preaches on the illegality of the court and the international powers destroying his small, independent country. In the BBC interview, Mira repeated his words – or perhaps Milošević was repeating her words at the Tribunal; it is hard to say. They both behave as people who have no doubt that they are in the right. And in the interview she reacted in exactly the same way as Milošević at the Tribunal: at first cool and composed, she became angrier and angrier (and consequently lisped more and more) as Tim Sebastian refused to accept her diatribes and insisted on proper answers. Obviously, she was not accustomed to such treatment and so she was shocked and put out: how dare he question her like that? Or rather, she was accustomed to communist-style journalism: a politician delivers a message, no questions asked. The press is there to spread that message or, as Mira puts it, 'the truth'.

But Milošević was in shock too. He did not believe that he could be arrested; he did not believe that he could be extradited to the International Tribunal; and he probably did not believe that he would ever actually be questioned. He was above all that. Both Mira Marković and Slobodan Milošević are used to preaching, not listening, to others. To offend them is to tell them to be quiet, to prevent them from talking. At the end of the interview, Mira tried another trick on Sebastian, the one she uses on her husband: feminine helplessness. In her most girlish voice she accused Tim Sebastian of not behaving towards her as a gentleman and a 'gallant knight'. It was an astonishing moment, because her use of the word 'knight' revealed the world she is living in – a fairy-tale world, populated by knights and dragons, by witches and fairies, and probably by princesses, too. In her world, knights show respect for ladies, and the prince and the princess live happily ever after.

Milošević and Mira's world is far removed from the outside world and impervious to reality. In his biography of Milošević entitled *On, ona i mi (Him, Her and Us)*, the Serbian journalist Slavoljub Djukić, writes that for Milošević and his wife 'reality has no importance at all'. Because they had power, they created their own reality; this is what power meant to them. They still see themselves not as they really are, but as they want each other to be – and want each other to see them. In other words, she is a brilliant intellectual, a great mind and his vulnerable little girl. He is a brilliant politician, a man of principles, a freedom fighter and her strong and capable husband. Now that the whole world is against them, they try even harder to shield each other from reality.

There is an air of tragedy about this couple. They may not have met with the same violent end as the Ceauşescus, but they suffer from the same affliction. They have no concept of the idea that people have to pay for their deeds, in one way or another. They refuse – or are perhaps unable – to understand why all this is happening to them. If reality does not adjust to their ideas – well then, so be it. So much the worse for reality – until reality finally, brutally, intruded into their lives.

Slobodan and Mira Milošević are truly like Hansel and Gretel. Unloved, abandoned but united in their own autistic world. When they wielded enormous power they were dangerous to everyone. Now they can harm only themselves.

11

Punished by the Gods

General Ratko Mladić, a commander of Republika Srpska forces, and Radovan Karadžić, the former President of Republika Srpska – the Serbian republic in Bosnia – have been charged by the Tribunal with crimes of genocide, crimes against humanity, grave breaches of the Geneva Convention, violations of the laws and customs of war, etc., in Bosnia between 1992 and 1995. As the result of these crimes, approximately two hundred thousand Bosnian Muslims lost their lives. Both men are also charged with occupation of the 'safe area' of Srebrenica and ordering summary executions of some seven thousand Muslim men. Mladić and Karadžić, considered the biggest war criminals after Slobodan Milošević, are still at large, and in hiding.

It was spring, and General Ratko Mladić was cutting roses in his garden in Belgrade. Cutting, pruning, mowing, watering – gardening had been his only occupation for some years now.

Seven years after the peace treaty in Bosnia, he was a general without an army, a man without a job. Nobody, except the Tribunal in The Hague, was interested in this 'Butcher of Bosnia'. When he was not occupied in his garden, attending a football match or eating at a restaurant, Mladić was drinking heavily. He frequently visited the graveyard where his daughter, Ana, was buried. Not yet sixty, Mladić was a psychological wreck. He no longer had anything to look forward to. He was a man of the war and the war was now the past.

Moreover, the new, post-Milošević Serbian government had deprived him of the bodyguards who once protected him. In 2002, following pressure on the Serbian government from The Hague to arrest him, he was forced to abandon his gardening and go into hiding.

Reality had finally caught up with him.

General Mladić fought at two fronts and lost on both of them. The first front was in Bosnia. After five years of fighting and conquering 70 per cent of Bosnian territory, he had to withdraw his troops according to the Dayton Agreement in November 1995. Republika Srpska got 49 per cent of Bosnian territory, but the Serbs from that territory were forced to live in an official federation together with Muslims and Croats.

The second front – of which he was perhaps not even aware – was in his own home. Because the real story about Mladić is not the one about his victories and losses on the battlefield. The real story about him is the one about his personal tragedy: his daughter's suicide. The fact that for years he had been a part of Serbian mythology could not help him when it came to his family. When Ana committed suicide in March 1994, his life turned from a classic Serbian myth into a classic Greek tragedy. It is the only time I have ever felt sorry for the man.

The night before his daughter's suicide Mladić's wife, Bosa, his son, Darko, and Ana were playing 'Sinking Ships' after dinner. This somehow moved me, reminding me of my own childhood, although Ana was a twenty-three-year-old medical student and Darko just a couple of years younger. 'Sinking Ships' is a children's game I used to play with my father when I was about eight, before there was television. After dinner my grandmother would bring out a box with all kinds of games, and we would sit and play until late at night. A radio would hum in the background. My father would be listening to the news, or we would all listen to the programme for seamen, in which mothers or wives requested their favourite songs – for Marko on his way to Singapore, or Peter on his way back from Costa Rica. My younger brother, who was too small to play with us, would sit in our grandma's lap and cheer for me. I loved these moments, when the whole family was engaged in the game, forgetting their daily grudges. But this was long ago, when I was a child.

I imagine that nostalgic scene being played in Mladić's house as well, the four of them sitting around the kitchen table. Jokes, Ana smiling, determined to win the game. Yet there is something strange about it, something that bothers me when I try to picture the scene. Something is wrong. Why would a brother and a sister, neither of them children any more, play a children's game with their parents?

Mladić is a stocky man with a big head and a bullneck. While he talks in the sharp, imposing voice of someone who is used to issuing commands, his reddish face glistens with sweat. His looks suggest that he enjoys earthly pleasures such as food and drink. He probably loves sausages, roasted piglet and lamb, *čevapčići*, and *sarma*, the latter two being Turkish specialities, of course, though one probably shouldn't point that out to him. But without what the Turks left behind in Serbia after five hundred years of occupation, there wouldn't be much in the way of Serbian cuisine. And a lot of food in Serbia is seasoned with hot red pepper, which calls for drinking *rakija*, the strong homemade local brandy distilled from plums. Every uniform must look too small on Mladić, as if it might burst at any moment. His red face indicates that his blood pressure is too high, and he probably suffers from high cholesterol. In short, he looks not so much like a soldier as a good candidate for a heart attack.

Yet it was not so long ago that his name was a synonym for fear to thousands of Muslims in Bosnia, so powerful was this man. Mladić was the person who kept Sarajevo besieged for three years, a city in which he had a house and where his mother and his friends used to live, a city that he knew well. Twelve thousand people were killed in Sarajevo before he withdrew his forces. Then he moved on to Gorazde and Srebrenica.

In Sarajevo, people who know him told me that he is a frightful person. It was General Mladić who made me understand how the fall of the UN-protected enclave of Srebrenica was possible – the fleeing of the Dutch UN corps, the days of massacre that followed, the exodus of some thirty thousand women and children.

I watched a documentary that showed his troops capturing Srebrenica on 11 July 1995, recorded by a Serbian television crew from his own TV-Pale. He is shown in a room negotiating with Colonel Tom Karremans, the UN Dutch battalion commander. Mladić stands facing the colonel, very dangerously close to him. He is perspiring heavily. Mladić is barking at Karremans: barking, not shouting. Because Mladić is much shorter than the colonel, he is barking even more loudly than necessary. Surrounded by his heavily armed soldiers, he is very convincing in making clear that Karremans and his 450 people are his prisoners.

In a badly lit hotel room in the village of Bratunac, Karremans repeats one particular gesture over and over again. He lifts his left hand to his throat and holds it there for a brief moment, as if having trouble breathing. After a couple of moments he does it again. And again. It appears an involuntary, compulsive movement, and the colonel is perhaps not even aware he is doing it. But he must feel something, perhaps mortal danger. He is a tall, slim man of about fifty, wearing uniform, and his face is frozen with fear. Leaning back against the wall of the hotel room, Tom Karremans touches his throat as if to protect it from being cut.

At one point in the documentary Mladić softens his tone a little and offers Karremans a cigarette. 'Do you smoke?' he asks. 'No, I don't,' Karremans says. 'Oh, take it, it's not your last one!' Mladić says laughing, recognising the other man's fear. The colonel has no choice but to take the cigarette. A while later Mladić asks him if he wants a glass of beer. Again, Karremans refuses. In order not to appear impolite or to offend the hostile Mladić, he even goes to the trouble of explaining that he doesn't think that he should drink alcohol because his soldiers are not allowed to drink. Mladić laughs wholeheartedly at him again: 'You will drink it, all right!' he says. And indeed Karremans will drink. The very next moment the colonel and Mladić are clinking glasses and drinking together.

When I see Karremans standing there in front of Mladić, so frightened that he is probably thinking, this is it, this is my end, I understand that he could not have defended anybody, not even himself. It is clear Karremans will obey Mladić, whatever he demands. Karremans is defeated, the UN troops are defeated, Srebrenica is defeated, and I read it all in the face of the Dutch commander.

The meeting of the two commanders, captured on camera, is an extraordinary document. Mladić deliberately humiliates the detained UN officer, who is not even an enemy but a neutral soldier. 'I want to help you,' he says to Karremans, 'although you don't deserve it, neither as a human being nor as an officer.' Mladić bullies him, insults him, threatens him in front of his soldiers and the TV camera. UN neutrality means nothing to him. He does not recognise the international intervention in what he considers to be his war. Foreigners only mess things up, as he says often.

The documentary reveals him as an aggressive, narcissistic person, full of himself after having taken the Srebrenica enclave. But it also shows Mladić as a liar. He lies to Karremans in telling him that the Muslim population is not the aim of his action. In Potocari, he tells thousands of exhausted women and children not to be afraid, nothing will happen to them, even though the buses that are to drive them away from their homes have already been ordered up. He also lies to a Muslim representative of Srebrenica who, at the mere sight of Mladić, is barely able to speak. Mladić tells him '. . . to all those who lay down their weapons I guarantee they will live. You have my word as a man and a general.'

This habit of lying practised by many Serbian politicians and army officers caused much confusion at the beginning of the war. Everybody lied: Milošević, Karadžić and Mladić. For a long time foreign negotiators took their promises at face value, only to realise later that they had been lied to. Obviously, they didn't have the same code of honesty. According to the Serbian understanding of the ethics of this war, lies were permitted in order to fool the enemy, to outsmart him. Indeed, it would be foolish to be truthful. Of course, Mladić did not intend to imprison Muslim soldiers who laid down their arms. In Srebrenica, Mladić did not take prisoners. After he gave his officer's word of honour that the prisoners would live, it was only a matter of hours before the executions began. The bloodbath that followed after 12 July was the biggest massacre in Europe since the Second World War, a massacre that would end the lives of 7,475 Muslim men from Srebrenica.

As a commander, Mladić had charisma and he knew it. Indeed, he was the most charismatic leader of them all. Among Serbs, just being a soldier carries a certain cachet. As a soldier, he was ascetic, disciplined, unafraid of the front line, not corrupted, not somebody eager to enrich himself on the black market. He rounded up Serbian peasants in Bosnia and made a proper army out of them. There are many anecdotes about him as a commander, but they all tell essentially the same story: he was not afraid of the enemy. Brutal and arrogant, convinced of his own military genius, he respected no one: not the international representatives, not the foreign commanders, not the press. Serbs from Republika Srpska, on the other hand, saw in him a father figure, somebody who protected and sheltered them. At the height of his career in 1995, Mladić was the most popular person in Republika Srpska, more popular than the President, Radovan Karadžić. At the same time he was the most hated and the most feared man in the Balkans, rivalling only Slobodan Milošević himself.

The Serbian press often compared Mladić to Prince Lazar Hrebljanović, the man who led the Serbian forces in the battle against the Turks at Kosovo Polje in 1389. According to legend, the day before the battle, the prophet Elijah flew from Jerusalem and appeared to Prince Lazar in the form of a grey falcon, offering him a choice: either he could win the battle and conquer a terrestrial kingdom, or he could lose the battle and gain a place in heaven for himself and his people. Prince Lazar did not hesitate. He chose to sacrifice his troops. And ever

since the day that battle was lost – 28 June, St Vitus' Day –
Serbs have considered themselves a 'celestial people', different
because they have chosen martyrdom.

This is the most powerful Serbian myth, one that,
surprisingly, is alive even today. Or, more accurately, it has
been revived, as Serbs, like any other nation, revive their
myths in difficult times. And now once again, after so many
centuries, the Serbs were fighting against Turks. They were not
the same Ottoman Turks from 1389, but they were Turks
nevertheless, or *balijas*, a derogatory name for the Bosnian
Muslims. This time the war was fought not at Kosovo Polje,
but in Bosnia. And once again it was lost. Nevertheless, like
the prince in the myth of the battle at Kosovo Polje, Mladić
became a 'celestial warrior', a mythological hero.

One could say that the history of the Serbian people is a
history of lost battles, but, according to the Kosovo myth,
defeat here means victory. In his first address to the nation
after his defeat by NATO in 1999, Slobodan Milošević, who
was then the President of the country, congratulated the Serbs
on their triumph. He did it in the best tradition of Kosovo
Polje, turning military defeat on earth into a spiritual victory.
Like Prince Lazar, given a choice between history and
mythology, Milošević chose the latter. But God did not
intervene in his case and Milošević survived the NATO
bombardments in 1999, an ordinary war criminal.

Interestingly enough, Milošević was never compared to
Prince Lazar. However, the general of the forces of
Republika Srpska, Ratko Mladić, was. Soldiers are better
material for mythological heroes, for epic poems and
martyrdom. Milošević was merely a politician, and politicians'
popularity comes and goes. He must still convince his people
that he is a mythological hero and that he was defending the
country from allied Western enemies, and he is trying to do

that at the Tribunal in The Hague. But Mladić, as a soldier, has already done it. In recent Serbian mythology, Mladić stands above Milošević.

On antique Serbian icons Prince Lazar is depicted as a thin, pale, spiritual man. There is nothing ethereal about Mladić. But he emanated power, and people were impressed by that. Mladić was very much aware of his 'celestial' fame, and he spoke as if from above: when one journalist dared ask Mladić who paid him and to whom he paid his taxes, Mladić gave him a heroic, 'celestial' answer: 'I don't work for money. My reward is the survival of my nation. There is no money that could pay me . . . The meaning of my life is to give to people what I could in these difficult times.'

His arrogance came as much from his character as from his situation, from living not so much in the real as in the mythological world. Even in his public speeches he could mix past and present in a single sentence. When he took Srebrenica, he said in front of a TV camera, 'I give this town to the Serbian people as a gift for St Vitus' Day. We finally took revenge on the Turks!' Some six hundred years after the battle at Kosovo Polje, General Mladić spoke about taking revenge on the Turks even though there were no longer any Turks in Bosnia. In his mythological world, Mladić, the archangel of Serbian revenge, finally brought justice to his people when he ordered the execution of thousands of 'Turks' (that is, Bosnian Muslims) in Srebrenica. In his mind, historical justice had finally been done.

That evening, as the Mladić family sat together around their table, there were no hints or premonitions of what was going to happen only twenty-four hours later. Ana had a headache that had been bothering her for some time, ever since she had come back from an excursion with her fellow students to

Moscow. She was one of the best medical students at the University of Belgrade and had almost finished her studies. The trip to Moscow was one traditionally taken by students in their last year. Her father was not pleased with the idea, but together mother and daughter somehow persuaded him to allow her to go, and so off she went.

When she returned, she was a different person. She started to complain about severe headaches and said she could not concentrate on her forthcoming exam. The oft-mentioned reason for her suicide is that she was finally confronted with the truth about the war. At some point perhaps she read something in the news, perhaps about what happened in Sarajevo. And for the first time Ana understood her father's role in the killings in Bosnia.

If it is true that this was the reason why Ana Mladić committed suicide, then I think I understand it. She could not confront him, could not demand an explanation or urge him to deny what she had read. Their family was a traditional, patriarchal family, and Ana had been taught never to challenge her father's authority. I know what that is like: my father was an officer, too. In our world such fathers often do not differentiate between their family and their soldiers; they do not talk, they issue commands. They don't expect anybody to contradict them, especially not about their work. I could never confront my father; I had to leave home to escape his overwhelming authority. In such a home there is no way for a child to ask his or her father about his job, even if it is evident that his job is to order the execution of civilians. Besides, Ana was not a man and, in spite of all his love for his daughter, when it came down to serious matters like war, a woman – if she was even present at such a discussion – should listen, not talk.

If she had dared that evening to say something to him, even to mention the war, he would have looked at her with his piercing blue eyes which would turn as cold as ice. A look of disbelief, then anger. Who was she to question him, her father? A general. Nobody would dare to address him in such a tone, not even foreign diplomats or his top commanders. My father's eyes were like that, and when he looked at me with those cold eyes I used to go weak at the knees. It was fear. I would look to my mother for help. But if I dared to answer my father back, if he had already given me that look and raised his voice, my mother would just watch us helplessly, as if paralysed. My mother never defended me and I could never forget that. Ana's mother would probably have done the same. Now, though my father is long dead, I still remember my helplessness in front of him and my mother's lost, submissive look.

Ana would have had to have been a very strong person to stand up to her father. Many times I have tried to imagine the conversation that might have taken place. She would, if she could, have asked him: Why? Why all these killings? He would answer her that she didn't understand, this was war and it was his job to defend his people. But what about women, children, old people? Why kill them, they were not soldiers? Muslims were killing children and women as well, he would answer. And for the first time he would realise that Ana was no longer his little girl, but a young woman with different values to her father, and this would shock him. Don't you believe me? he would ask her. No, I don't, she would say. Her response would infuriate him and he would start to shout, forgetting that he was not among his soldiers.

Or perhaps she would ask him if all that she had read about him was true: did he really order the killing of thousands of civilians in Sarajevo? Mladić would deny everything, would accuse her of believing 'enemy propaganda'. Lying to his own daughter would come easy to him; he had lied to others so many times before. It would nevertheless frustrate him that his own daughter dared challenge him.

But imagining this conversation is wrong. Because if Ana and her father had been able to talk to each other, she wouldn't be dead now. He will never, as long as he lives – and this is also a part of his suffering – be able to understand why Ana killed herself. And the answer lies in their game of 'Sinking Ships': of two young grown-up people sitting with their parents and playing a children's game with them rather than watching television or going out with their friends. Ana and Darko probably wanted to do something else, but they knew their father all too well, his whims and silly requests. It was he who had demanded they play with him because it was his way of relaxing. They could not refuse him. He loved to have his family around him and to play some innocent game – as if nothing else of importance was happening, as if there was no war going on, as if all was well as long as the four of them were sitting around the table playing childish games.

As they played that night, Ana must have known everything. Days earlier she had read articles about her father. Before that, like many of her friends, she had avoided dealing with the war. She was aware that her father was a popular commander-in-chief of the troops of Republika Srpska, and she was proud of him, but she did not know and did not want to know that his job was 'ethnic cleansing'. Until it became inevitable. Until it was too late to face up to it and survive.

So there she sat playing, even joking that she was going to win. The general's favourite game of 'Sinking Ships' was not so innocent of course: it is a military game. Even at his own kitchen table Mladić couldn't escape what he was and who he was. That evening Ana again complained about her headache. But the signal was not clear enough, because she said nothing else, nothing more. You are probably getting flu, her mother said, touching her forehead lightly. Her father looked at her worriedly, but said nothing.

No, I won't say anything to my father, Ana probably thought. It would be impossible, she had already gone over it many times. She didn't have the strength to destroy this family idyll. She couldn't do that, not in front of her mother and her little brother. Her mother would become pale and speechless. Her brother would jump to her defence if their father started shouting or perhaps tried to hit her. The evening before her suicide, she looked at him differently. Her father was no longer the same person to her. Her headache was real, but it was only an excuse for withdrawing. The truth was that she couldn't bear to look at him any more.

Suddenly she felt nauseated. She looked at him, at the 'Butcher of Bosnia' (she had read in some newspapers that this was his nickname), as if seeing him for the first time. Ana looked at her father, at his big hands, his favourite ring, his already very grey hair, and a feeling of sadness overwhelmed her, a feeling of loss. Was it possible that she was sitting opposite a man accused of war crimes and saying nothing? And that this person was her father, her beloved father? Was it possible that he was so hard, so cynical, so inhuman? He smiled at her. She smiled back, a vague, little smile, and made a move, sinking one of his ships. She hated herself for being so weak, so squeamish, Daddy's little girl. The headache got stronger. I have to go to bed, she said. Her mother looked at her. She sensed that something was wrong with her daughter, but just how wrong she didn't know.

The lamp cast a circle of yellowish light on the family kitchen table. The game was almost over. Ana had won.

Ana had one more chance in the morning. Mladić was really worried about her and finally asked her what the matter was. She said only that she couldn't explain her behaviour. He left

Belgrade for Bosnia, sure that her strange mood would soon lift, that she was nervous and worried about the forthcoming exam.

The following night Ana took her father's pistol, one of three that he kept in their house, the special one that had been given to him as an award for being the best student of the Military Academy in Belgrade – the one that Mladić had told Ana that he would fire to salute the birth of his first grandson. She took that one, as if she wanted to hurt her father even more.

Away in Bosnia with his soldiers, at the moment his daughter killed herself the general was awakened from his sleep. He felt a blow in his heart, he said later. He told his orderly that something terrible must have happened and that he should immediately call the front line. But the front line was quiet. Then the telephone rang. It was his son.

Mladić was convinced that Ana had been murdered. This, to him, was the only logical explanation. Ana would never kill herself. He could not conceive that his daughter, his own daughter who played 'Sinking Ships' with him at twenty-three, could condemn him for what he had done. He could not understand it. Instead of talking, they were playing a children's game. To think she had been murdered was easier for him: it relieved him of all responsibility. To understand why she committed suicide would mean that he would have to admit – at least to himself – that, indeed, he had committed war crimes. This General Mladić could never do. Not even the death of his beloved child could make him acknowledge it. It was as if he had to sacrifice his own daughter – not his soldiers and his own life, as Prince Lazar had – in order to become a mythological hero. If this was the price for his immortality, the gods left him alive only to make him endure the incredible pain.

At this point, Serbian mythology meets Greek tragedy: Mladić was punished for what he did in Bosnia. He destroyed Bosnia, but ultimately Bosnia finished him. If Ana had been killed by a human hand, by the hand of an enemy, that would have been a human revenge. But the hand had been her own. The gods took revenge on Mladić. His life was like a Greek tragedy in which the gods intervene in the hero's life and punish him for his hubris while he is still alive. Mladić finally experienced the pain that he had inflicted on thousands of people in Sarajevo, Srebrenica and Gorazde. But could it be the same pain? Can a butcher experience the same feelings as his victims? Yes, because the pain of a parent who has lost his child is a universal one.

This loss, Mladić's greatest loss and the suffering that went with it, turned him from a mythological hero into a human being again.

After I left home, at just sixteen years old, my father did not speak to me for years. He was as hard as stone. He wrote me off. Why? I often wondered. Because I dared to do things on my own and not listen to him. But perhaps I would have listened to him, if only he had talked to me, talked rather than shouted. It is too late now. But I often dream about my father. I dream that I am standing at the top of a spiral staircase. My father is at the bottom of it. He is looking up at me and seems to be trying to tell me something. I see his mouth moving, but no words reach me. I wake up sobbing.

Perhaps the general, too, dreams about his lost daughter who is trying to tell him something that he cannot hear. Then he wakes up in a cold sweat, next to his silent wife, who deep down knows all too well who is responsible for Ana's suicide.

This is why, as of March 1994, General Mladić has been serving his life sentence, regardless of the fact that he is a war criminal sought by the Tribunal in The Hague who is still on the run.

12

The Metamorphosis of Biljana Plavšić

Not many women took part in the war, especially at the top level. Biljana Plavšić was one of the three highest-ranking officials in Republika Srpska during the war, next to Radovan Karadžić and Momčilo Krajišnik – both indicted by the Tribunal. Plavšić was sentenced to eleven years in prison for crimes against humanity, violations of the laws and customs of war and grave breaches of the Geneva Convention. She is one of the very few war criminals to have acknowledged her own responsibility.

The only woman accused of war crimes, the 'iron lady' of Republika Srpska sits calmly in the dock of the Tribunal in The Hague. It is February, it is cold, and she is dressed in an elegant black suit and an olive-green turtleneck pullover, with a big cross hanging from a chain around her neck. From time to time she rests her chin pensively on one hand or fidgets nervously in her chair. But when Judge Richard May reads her sentence – eleven years in prison – Biljana Plavšić does not change the expression on her face. For the seventy-two-year-old, eleven years of imprisonment could mean the rest of her life. Yet, she looks directly into the judge's eyes, unflinching. Composed, calm and solemn, she maintains her poise. No one can guess what is she thinking.

Biljana Plavšić looks very good for her age. Her greyish hair is cut to shoulder length and she wears very little make-up, only some mascara for her eyelashes and discreet lipstick. Pastel or jewel-toned outfits are her usual form of dress, her trademarks. Pale green, lavender, fuchsia and dark blue seem to be her favourite colours, a silk shirt under her jacket part of her uniform.

I must admit that, in the circumstances, Biljana Plavšić looks impeccable. One photograph of her in particular captures this very well: it shows her visiting soldiers in the field, her cheerful pink suit standing out among camouflage uniforms, just as surely as her feminine appearance stands out among rough male faces. Nothing could have contrasted more with the uniforms than her bright coloured apparel *à la* Chanel, except perhaps an evening dress. She looks as if she doesn't belong there, not because she is a woman, but because she is a lady.

This is how she looks in the courtroom, too: as if she doesn't belong there.

Her attitude in the court has been described as dignified. I agree; in the courtroom she does look dignified, but her dignity verges on arrogance. There is something about the way she sits there, something about her bearing, the way she turns her head when she looks at the judges, as if from above, as if *she* should be judging *them*. It bothers me, her air of superiority.

Biljana Plavšić irritates me until I recognise something very familiar about her – or does she irritate me only because I recognise it? She reminds me of my mother. My mother intimidates people just by being who she is, even today at seventy-six years old. And it has nothing to do with her power or her position, because she has never had either. When I was young, I never liked inviting my friends to our house because of my mother. She was considered cold and haughty, even arrogant, because of the way she held herself, as if she thought herself a queen. It now strikes me that Plavšić must be the same type of woman. Some people seem to have an inbred dignified or arrogant attitude (it all depends on the interpretation). Such people make you feel uneasy, make you feel as if something is wrong with you: you have messy hair or a mark on your dress or you've said something stupid. It's not that they want to make you feel that way, it's just the way they are and, because of it, they seem to disregard people, often unaware that they are doing so. Some foreign diplomats have described Plavšić as cold and unpleasant, noting that other Serbian politicians were warm and forthcoming, while she would not even shake hands with them.

In fact, while sitting in the courtroom, Plavšić looks exactly as she used to before she launched herself into high politics: a distinguished professor. More precisely, she was an accomplished professor of biology at the University of Sarajevo who spent some time in the United States on a Fulbright scholarship. It is hard to say what made her leave her profession. Probably, as in most cases, the answer is banal: the lust for power. But I can easily imagine what her situation looked like in 1990 just before the war in Bosnia broke out. She was sixty years old and heading for retirement. Ambitious and intelligent, she was not attracted by that prospect. She had no husband and no children or grandchildren to devote her time to. More importantly, she saw the kind of people who entered politics. A few of them were her colleagues, academics like

Nikola Koljević, a well-known expert on Shakespeare (who committed suicide in 1997). But most of them were rather uncultured, semi-literate men with no ambition except to profit personally from being in power. Of course she thought that she could be a better and more competent politician than them. With no family obligations and plenty of energy, she threw herself into politics. She was certainly driven by ambition, but, unlike her male colleagues, she seems to have remained uncorrupted. One should not forget that, when she realised how much corruption there was in her government, she started an anti-corruption purge and formed a party of her own which won the elections in 1997.

But there was a price to pay for being the only woman among those macho Balkan politicians. A woman in such a position had to be far better than the men, and, under the circumstances, for Biljana Plavšić, that meant she had to be more radical in her rhetoric. And she was.

The fact that a woman could be responsible for some of the most appalling atrocities committed in Bosnia during the war must be hard to swallow for anyone who believes – even vaguely – that if women ruled, the world would be a better place. When this woman ruled Bosnia, it was pure hell.

In Republika Srpska, she was formally second only to the President, Radovan Karadžić. It is hard to say how much power she really had and how much she was manipulated by Slobodan Milošević and Radovan Karadžić, if she was not there simply to be decorative. 'She had never been brought into any of the discussions, any of the decisions and any of the meetings to deal with the critical issues of war, peace and power,' said Carl Bildt, the former international High Representative in Bosnia, when testifying at her trial. But even if she had little power, she knew what was going on, and in court she did not deny it.

Because she is a woman, I found it difficult to follow Biljana Plavšić over the decade of her political career. It was painful to listen to her hard-core nationalist speeches and her metaphors borrowed from biology, as when she tried to explain that Muslims in Bosnia were a 'genetic mistake on the Serbian body' and that to eliminate them was a 'natural phenomenon' – not a war crime. Even Slobodan Milošević considered her too radical, deeming her fit for the madhouse. It was terrible to think that she, as one of the formal heads of the secret police of Republika Srpska, as well as the one of the military commanders, must have been aware of the starvation, torture and killing of Muslim prisoners in the appalling concentration camps of Omarska, Keraterm and Manjača. Another photograph of her from the war shows her kissing the notorious criminal Željko Ražnatović Arkan hours after his Serbian paramilitary troops had entered Bijeljina and killed forty-eight people. The corpses were still lying in the streets – indeed, she had to step over one body in order to throw her arms around Arkan's neck, kiss him and congratulate him on the successful elimination of the 'genetic mistake'.

When she heard that she had been indicted, she immediately surrendered herself to the Tribunal in January 2001, firmly believing that she had fulfilled her duty in defending her people and therefore could not be guilty of genocide, crimes against humanity, violations of the laws and customs of war and breaches of the Geneva Convention, with which she was charged by the International Criminal Tribunal for the former Yugoslavia. Indeed, her first statement in front of the Tribunal was the usual 'not guilty' plea.

After spending a short period of time in prison, she was released on bail. But the real shock was caused by a video-link declaration in October 2002 when Plavšić, for the very first time, changed her original statement and confessed her guilt.

This caused consternation among many Serbs: what was the matter with the woman? What did she hope to achieve? Speculation was rife. Perhaps she was looking for a reduced sentence in exchange for testifying against Milošević? After all, she was known as a cool and calculating person, and such deals with the prosecutors and the court itself were part of juridical practice and could not be ruled out.

But Biljana Plavšić surprised us all. When she was given the chance to speak at the Tribunal in December the same year, she cut the picture of a person altogether different from the one we had seen before. So different, in fact, that she was unrecognisable. In her short address she was sincere, modest, moving and full of remorse.

It is nothing less than a miracle that, once on trial, Biljana Plavšić did not say, *I did not know*, did not say, *I was only doing my job*, and did not try to evoke sympathy because she was the only woman in that Balkan world of male politicians. She had by now changed her plea to guilty for crimes against humanity (and, in response, the prosecution dropped the rest of the charges against her). 'I am convinced and I accept that several thousand innocent people were victims of organised and systematic actions to remove Muslims and Croats from a territory that Serbs consider to be theirs,' she said to the court. And that statement is unprecedented.

To the question that she herself posed – how was it possible that Serbs could commit war crimes? – her answer was: blinding fear, which led to the obsessive determination never to become victims again, as the Serbs had been during the Second World War when civil war raged between them and Croats. 'In this obsession not to become victims ever again, we allowed ourselves to become perpetrators,' she admitted. However, she did not bother to note that this latent fear dating back to the Second World War had been whipped up by the media and, years before any fighting broke out, prepared the collective mind-set to allow the crimes that would follow.

Confronted with the accusation of inhuman treatment of non-Serbs, she confirmed that she had heard about it, but did not check whether or not it was true, because at that time she believed that her people could not be capable of such deeds. But she conceded that the notion of self-defence is no excuse for war crimes, and she now accepted her full responsibility. Her words acknowledging guilt are important also because she is the first – and so far the only – political or military leader at the International Tribunal to accept her responsibility.

In her short plea, Plavšić also found a way to appeal to the judges to seek justice for the victims and for all three sides in the war. 'I can only do what is in my power and hope that it will be of some use – to understand the truth, to say it and to accept responsibility. This, I hope, will help innocent Muslim, Croat and Serbian victims not to be dominated by bitterness that often turns into hatred, which, at the end, leads to self-destruction.' Her aim was not to get a milder sentence because, as she later put it, any sentence of more than ten years in her case would mean the remainder of her life. But she refused to cooperate with the Tribunal by appearing as a prosecution witness in other trials, especially that of Milošević.

Her speech must be seen as more than an act of personal courage. It is historical for the simple reason that, following her admission that Serbs were perpetrators, nobody can deny it any longer, not when it comes from someone at such a high level, from the top brass. Her words might therefore have serious consequences for the process of 'sobering up' the vast majority of Serbs who have not yet even started to articulate their responsibility for the war. This, at least, was the hope at the ICTY in The Hague. But back in Republika Srpska and in

Serbia, the first reaction to her guilty plea was unexpected: her plea was condemned and she was pronounced a traitor. It will take more than her trial to force the Serbs to deal with their role in the war in Bosnia.

But Biljana Plavšić still proved herself a person of some moral stamina and strength, prepared to accept the consequences of her deeds. Facing her judges, she demonstrated a remarkable readiness to accept her punishment. Her behaviour is admirable, even I have to admit that.

As she was once the most radical person in the government of Republika Srpska, so she is now the most radical one in remorse. During the war perhaps she had to be more militant than the men surrounding her in order to be considered their equal. Of course, the interesting question is, what made her change her mind now?

Plavšić herself has given us no answers. However, there are some clues. In her address, Biljana Plavšić mentioned the loss of honour of the Serbian people because of the war crimes they committed. And then she went on to talk about the role that St Sava occupies in Serbian history. The Serbian leadership had departed from the saint's path of respect, nobility and honour, she said. But why, one asks, would she cite a medieval saint? The answer might be contained in what is most visible when one takes a closer look at her in the courtroom: the cross hanging ostentatiously from her neck, for everybody to see. There is no doubt that it is a statement. Could it be that her religious belief made her change her mind? Or was it something completely different that made her confess her guilt – her rational scientist's mind? Faced with unquestionable proof in the court, she changed her mind, as every true scientist would do, in spite of ideology. Her rationality, it seems to me, could be proved by the fact that she really contributed to the realisation of the Dayton Agreement in 1995, that she confronted the rampant corruption, and that she cooperated with international organisations afterwards.

Whatever it was that brought about her moral metamorphosis, Biljana Plavšić not only set a positive example, but she also delivered a lecture in patriotism to her male colleagues, to war criminals like Radovan Karadžić and Ratko Mladić, and to Croatian 'heroes' like Ante Gotovina hiding somewhere in Herzegovina. While he skulks like a coward, she, a woman, had the courage to admit her own personal guilt, thereby trying to rid her own people of the prejudice that every Serb must be guilty simply by definition.

This must be a hard, even humiliating lesson, for men to take from a woman in a society as patriarchal as our Balkan one. Men like Karadžić, Mladić and Gotovina will not forgive her for exposing them as even more miserable figures than they already were.

13

Why We Need Monsters

'Why are you writing about war criminals?' a friend asked me when I told her that I would be going to The Hague for five months to follow trials at the International Criminal Tribunal for the former Yugoslavia. I understood her question; she meant: haven't you had enough of all that?

Yes, I had. When I finished my last novel, *As If I Am Not There* – my second book about the war in the Balkans – I was very, very tired of the war. Year after year, for ten years, I had tried to understand and explain to others the reason for the war, how it came about and how it unmistakably changed people around me, myself included. I wanted to write about something else for a change. But my thoughts kept coming back to the war. I simply could not put it behind me yet; there were too many questions, too many loose ends. The 1991–5 war was something that I, like many others, could never have imagined. I never thought it possible in Yugoslavia, and I had to come to terms with it in some way. Writing was one way. But writing two books about war was not enough. After all, that war changed my life. Confronted with nationalism, my daughter left Croatia in 1991 to live abroad. I lost the country of my birth and many of my friends. My world shrank to an almost homogenous Croatia. Excommunicated from its public life, I spent more and more time abroad, until finally I found myself living in Sweden, my second homeland now.

Nevertheless, the war would not leave me alone. A few years ago I gave a reading in Berlin from my novel *As If I Am Not There*, which was about mass rapes of Muslim women in Bosnia. As usual, after the reading there was a discussion with the audience. A young man stood up and asked me if I would consider writing a book from the perspective of a perpetrator now. 'No, I will not!' I answered almost too eagerly, as if doing so would be a crime. True, my books about the war were written from the perspective of victims only. The horror of the war could truly be described only from their position, I thought. The world already knew enough about the perpetrators. How many articles had been written about Slobodan Milošević? Thousands. In time, thanks to the media, Slobodan Milošević, Radovan Karadžić and Ratko Mladić had practically become celebrities; whatever their crimes had been, it was no longer remembered or even important. If one attempts to write from the point of view of the perpetrators, to try to understand such people, how close does it come to justifying their acts? Can we actually understand war criminals? More importantly, why should we even try? These were the questions that went through my mind as I thought about how ominous it was that this subject should be brought up in Germany of all places.

I did not realise at the time that, in response to a young German reader's inquiry, I had reacted in a typically self-defensive way. Exactly in the same way as when, two years later, other people would react when I told them that I was writing about perpetrators, i.e. war criminals. Why are you interested in them? They are monsters, they'd say.

It is easy to understand such reactions. War criminals have committed indescribable acts and nobody wants to be connected to them in any way. But this doesn't bring us closer to the essential question: how were such crimes possible? If we believe their perpetrators are monsters, it is because we wish to create as great a distance as possible between us and them, to exclude them from humanity altogether. We even go so far as to say that their crimes were 'inhuman', as if evil (as well as good) were not a part of human nature. At the bottom of such reasoning there is a syllogism: ordinary people could not do what these monsters did. We are ordinary people, therefore we cannot commit such crimes.

But once you get closer to the real people who committed those crimes, you see that the syllogism doesn't really work.

In 1993 I followed the trial of Borislav Herak, a Serb from Bosnia who was sentenced to death (later changed to life imprisonment) by a court in Sarajevo for sixteen rapes and the murder of thirty-two civilians (twelve of them raped women) and for his participation in the killing of some 220 Muslims. My biggest disappointment was finding that this was a man who looked like any other: a neighbour, a relative or even a friend. I looked almost desperately for a trace of madness in his eyes, for any evidence that he was different – in short, that he was a monster. And I was not the only person looking for such signs in war criminals. Many have done the same.

Does some personality flaw – or a specific type of character – cause human cruelty or not? Is there in every community a certain percentage of people who have the pathology to commit the worst crimes if they are given a chance? Or do they commit crimes under social and psychological pressure? These questions are not new. There is a whole library of competently written books about this issue, many of which appeared just after the Second World War (for example, by Raul Hilberg, Theodor Adorno, Zygmunt Bauman, John Steiner and Ervin Staub). But as we are newly confronted with such cases, the questions about the nature of their behaviour are as disturbing now as ever.

Surely there are cases bordering on the pathological (Goran Jelisić being one), but the quantity and brutality of crimes committed (mass rapes in Bosnia, for example) suggests that either the number of sick people is rather large, or something else is at work. In his book *Ordinary Men* the American historian Christopher Browning analyses the case of the 101st Reserve Battalion and the 'final solution' in Poland. He concludes that those Germans who were sent first to kill thousands of Polish Jews were not specially chosen or in any way different from other Germans. On the contrary, their battalion was composed of people from all walks of life and in that way was truly representative of 'ordinary men'.

An unemployed twenty-two-year-old, Borislav Herak was not interested in politics, nor did he personally hate Muslims. But when he was given a chance to kill them on apparently legitimate grounds and, in addition, to enrich himself by looting his victims, he did not think twice. What was frightening about watching Herak on trial was realising that he was neither a nationalist nor a madman – although intelligence was not one of his stronger points.

But if there was something in his character that made him behave pathologically (and I don't deny that there may be such cases), there is no more reason for us to occupy ourselves with Herak and others like him than to study exotic insects in the Amazon. Such cases tell us only that there are people who are mad or sick and whose behaviour has no consequence for ordinary people who are not similarly afflicted.

The more I have occupied myself with the individual cases of war criminals, the less I believe them to be monsters. What if they are ordinary people, just like you and me, who found themselves in particular circumstances and made the wrong moral decisions? What might this tell us about *ourselves*?

You sit in a courtroom watching a defendant day after day and at first you wonder, as Primo Levi did, 'If this is a man'. No, this is not a man, it is all too easy to answer, but as the days pass you find the criminals become increasingly human. Soon you feel you know them intimately. You watch their faces, ugly or pleasant, the way they yawn, take notes, scratch their heads or clean their nails, and you have to ask yourself: what if this *is* a man? The more you know them, the more you wonder how they could have committed such crimes – these waiters and taxi drivers, teachers and peasants in front of you. And the more you realise that war criminals might be ordinary people, the more afraid you become. Of course, this is because the consequences are more serious than if they were monsters. If ordinary people committed war crimes, it means that any of us could commit them. Now you understand why it is so easy and comfortable to accept that war criminals are monsters, rather than to agree with Ervin Staub that 'evil that arises out of ordinary thinking and is committed by ordinary people is the norm, not the exception'.

Indeed, it seems to me that brutality in war is more the norm than the exception, and more to do with circumstances than with character. But if this is really the case, none of us can be sure how we would behave in those particular circumstances. In short, there are no guarantees, as numerous psychological tests have proven. For example, in his famous 1971 Stanford Prison simulation experiment in inducing pain on command, Philip Zimbardo found that within only a few days the 'guards' became so sadistic he had to abandon the experiment. 'How could intelligent, mentally healthy, "ordinary" men become perpetrators of evil so quickly?' he asked. As frightening as this idea is, it is precisely the reason we should learn more about extraordinary situations and ordinary people's reactions to them. This is why we need to learn more about perpetrators and how they came to be. The young German reader was right. Only if we understand that most perpetrators are people like us can we see that we too might one day be in danger of succumbing to the same kind of pressure.

Yet, one question remains: what happens to make that ordinary man see an enemy in a colleague or a neighbour? How is it possible for hatred, humiliation, brutality and even murder to become legitimate behaviour? One soldier from the 101st Reserve Battalion admitted that to his unit Jews were not human beings. But what political, social and psychological processes in a society make such thinking possible? What makes mass hatred possible, and what makes possible the 'ethnic cleansing' that it engenders?

Perhaps it is far-fetched to compare Nazi Germany with any part of the former Yugoslavia. But one element makes such a comparison feasible, and that is the construction of the 'Other' as the object of hatred. To begin with, it is important to identify that object and give compelling reasons for hatred. The reasons do not have to be rational or even necessarily true. The most important thing is that they are convincing, because this makes them acceptable to people. Such 'explanations' are usually based on myths (the myth of Serbs as a 'celestial people', for example, or the myth about the Croatians' thousand-year-old dream of having their own state) and prejudices (Serbs are primitive, Croats are Nazis, Muslims are stupid). But it helps if these myths and prejudices are rooted in reality, either in the history of earlier wars or in cultural and religious differences.

As we still see in many parts of the world, the object of hatred could also be people belonging to another tribe (as, in

Rwanda, the Hutus and Tutsis), or of a different race. The task of propaganda is to shape this difference so that it creates a feeling of threat from the other side and strengthens the urge for homogenisation. Most important is the method of introducing hatred: it is most effective if people get used to it slowly, step by step, until they have absorbed it into their daily life.

In light of the 'evidence' of differences, often in the form of detailed descriptions of pressures and suffering in the mass media – either real or invented – in time those 'Others' are stripped of all their individual characteristics. They are no longer acquaintances or professionals with particular names, habits, appearances and characters; instead they are members of the enemy group. When a person is reduced to an abstraction in such a way, one is free to hate him because the moral obstacle has already been abolished. If it has been 'proved' that our enemies are no longer human beings, we are no longer obliged to treat them as such. It doesn't count at all that by doing so we are reducing ourselves to an abstract category as well, that we are no longer individuals because in the eyes of 'the enemy' we are the 'Others', too.

The beginning of the war in the former Yugoslavia did not differ from what Victor Klemperer wrote in *I Shall Bear Witness*, his diary from 1933 to 1941, when he described how, little by little, anti-Semitism became a normal way of thinking and behaving in Germany at that time. This perception comes slowly also to the victim: Klemperer, himself a Jew, did not want to see it and brushed it aside for years.

As in Germany, in Croatia you first stopped greeting a person of the other nationality, perhaps only because you were afraid that others would see you acknowledging him. Unbelievable as it is, this seemingly insignificant concession, this small act of adaptation to a new reality of the total national homogenisation, set you on a dangerous road. Turning your face the other way in fact created the opportunity for someone else to commit war crimes in the name of the very same principles of isolation and elimination of the 'Others'.

Most people in Croatia, Serbia and Bosnia adjusted to a mixture of state propaganda, opportunism, fear and indifference that created a norm of behaviour, without being properly aware of the consequences. Very few people were able to resist the general atmosphere of the 'normality of hatred'. Of course, there is a difference between a person who does not greet a Serb or a Muslim neighbour and a man who kills him – just as there is a difference between a government that does not issue documents to Serbs and one that orders the wearing of yellow stars. But turning your head away or remaining silent in the face of injustice and crime means collaborating with a politics whose programme is death and destruction. And whether it is willing or unwilling collaboration doesn't really matter, because the result is the same.

More than a decade after the beginning of the war in the Balkans, it is essential that we understand that it is we ordinary people and not some madmen who made it possible. We were the ones who one day stopped greeting those neighbours of a different nationality – an act that the next day made possible the opening of concentration camps. We did it to each other. Maybe this is a good reason for considering whether or not it is too easy to put a hundred men on trial in The Hague. What about the others who embraced the ideology that led to the deaths of two hundred thousand people? Perhaps they did not believe in it, but certainly they did not protest against it. If it is true that there is no collective guilt, can there be collective innocence?

Often in Croatia one heard it said that the Tribunal was trying not merely a few war criminals but the defensive 'war for the Homeland' and the whole Croat nation as well. In other words, guilt is not individualised. We are still prisoners of collectivism. Guilt needs individualisation, which is exactly what the Tribunal stands for. A whole nation, Croat or other, could not be held *guilty* of war crimes. But the whole nation could indeed be held *responsible* for war crimes, both politically and morally. The people in Serbia voted Slobodan Milošević in as President of Serbia twice and as President of Yugoslavia once. Croats voted Franjo Tudjman in as President on two occasions. To our knowledge these were reasonably free elections. If Germans were responsible for supporting Hitler, why should not Serbs be responsible for supporting Milošević and Croats for supporting Tudjman? Neither of them could have survived in power without the support of the people.

In voting for Milošević or Tudjman, people voted for the politics of 'ethnic cleansing'. Could they claim, like the Germans, that they did not know? Both Croatia and Serbia are too small to use that as an argument. During the five years of war, too many people were directly involved in ethnic cleansing to be able to claim seriously that they 'did not know'. They knew and they went along with it, or at least they did not care about it. This is the main reason they don't like to talk about war crimes, or about war in general, except for the notion of the heroic defensive war. It is not pleasant to learn that you were a collaborator. But it is necessary to learn that you had a choice – and that you made the wrong one. In some way, not only the war criminals but also people who made them possible should be held responsible for their wrong choices, too.

The trials of war criminals are important not only because of those killed. They are important also because of the living. In the end, what matters with regard to war criminals, and why we should bother to take a closer look at them, is one single important question: what would I do in their situation? The unpleasant truth is that there is no clear answer.

Brotherhood and Unity

It is a day like any other in the Scheveningen detention unit in The Hague. While Goran Jelisić and Tihomir Blaškić are walking in the courtyard, Rahim Ademi is cooking lunch. His wife, who recently visited him, brought him some food from Croatia: Dalmatian prosciutto, olive oil and fresh fish from the Adriatic. Fish from the North Sea tastes different: they all agree about that. It is fat and has no taste, especially when it is boiled and then served with a thick sauce, as is the custom here in the Netherlands. Could it be that there is too little salt in the North Sea?

But now, thanks to Ademi, the whole floor smells enticingly of today's meal, which is *brodetto*, a kind of fish stew. Ademi is the best cook of the twelve who live on this floor. Earlier it was another Croat, Dario Kordić, who often attended to their meals, but since Ademi arrived he has practically taken over. He can make a most delicious beef stroganoff and Viennese schnitzel, not to mention scampi in tomato sauce or calamari stuffed with garlic, a lot of parsley, breadcrumbs and the finely chopped tentacles of the squid.

Everybody agrees that his lamb chops, marinated with rosemary, thyme and sage, are excellent. Even his ordinary chicken soup tastes better than anything they get from the common kitchen in their detention unit.

The food that they get in the Scheveningen detention unit is, of course, something different: pale, meagre, lacking in any particular flavour or smell. More like the food you would get in hospital, although most of these men are reasonably healthy, and when they say 'hospital' they mean one of those ragged hospitals in the country they all come from. They crave the food they are used to: a good beef soup with handmade, thinly cut noodles, pitta with young cheese or a loaf of crusty, warm bread, roasted meat, *sarma*, and the famous *čevapčići* or *ražnjići*. And a bottle of good Dalmatian wine to go with it – but they don't get this. No alcohol is permitted.

Of course, nobody here minds if the meal is Bosnian or Serbian or Croatian; they are not nationalists when it comes to good food. They are just happy every time they get freshly made, tasty meals. Fortunately they can order food to be brought in from outside. So every Monday a list is made, carefully, to accommodate everyone's wishes and tastes. If there is a holiday or a birthday or some other occasion to celebrate, they can order a whole lamb or a piglet and roast it, just as they would do back home. And they eat it together, enjoying every morsel of it. As they did when the detention unit's management decided to hold a seasonal party for all of them in an effort to unite them even more. It was just like during the days of communism, when instead of Christmas it was the New Year that was celebrated. The official celebration was on 19 December, and celebrations of the Catholic and Orthodox Christmases and the Muslim holidays were allowed, too. The detainees roasted a whole piglet. The atmosphere was, in the words of Timothy McFadden, an Irish army officer and the

Director of the Scheveningen detention unit (he doesn't like it
being called a prison, and rightly so since it is a separate unit
within the Scheveningen prison), 'very pleasant, very jolly . . .
lots of salads and cooked meats and bread and what do you call
it . . . *baklava*? . . . and plenty of music playing, that typically
Yugoslavian or Balkan music. Well, I don't know which is the
correct way to say it now.'

In the common room Sefer Halilović is reading newspapers
from Bosnia that have just arrived. They all follow only what
is happening back home, even if they aren't sure when, if ever,
they will return there. After Halilović has finished, Blaškić,
Naletilić Tuta, Kvočka and the others will read the same
newspapers. They all read the very same newspapers
regardless of which part of former Yugoslavia they happen to
come from. Language is the other thing besides food that
unites them all. Like refugees scattered across continents, they
usually do not specify; they call it 'our language' or nothing at
all. No name is needed. Of course they each have their own
language, but why should they complicate life even further by
naming them as long as they understand each other without
doing so? The fact is that it makes no difference if they speak
Serbian, Croatian or Bosnian – they all understand each other
perfectly. And where language is concerned, these men show
no sign of nationalism. Except in the courtroom, sometimes.
But that is more for the records: for example, during his trial
Dario Kordić complained that the translation was not in the
Croatian but in the Serbian language. He did not say that he
did not understand it, only that it was not his language.
Blagoje Simić remarked that he recognised some Croatian
words in his simultaneous translation into Serbian. But these
instances were exceptions.

Some of the men work out in the gym – a very popular
place among the detainees – while others are in the Tribunal.

Slobodan Milošević is working in his office. He has an extra cell at his disposal because officially he has no lawyer and is taking care of his own defence, although he is unofficially helped by a whole crew of lawyers working for him in Belgrade. After lunch he will probably join other detainees from his floor – Radislav Krstić, Paško Ljubičić and Dragoljub Prcać among them – in the common room and perhaps play gin rummy with them, if he is not too tired; lately one can see that his trial is wearing on him. When he was first brought in, the governors of Scheveningen feared that the other detainees would react aggressively towards Milošević and therefore kept him in isolation. Indeed, some days after his arrival, Goran Jelisić punched Milošević (of course, the two men could not be kept on the same floor afterwards). But Milošević's isolation did not last long, as it was soon clear that, except for Jelisić, the others accepted him as one of them. Soon he was sharing meals and newspapers with the rest of the detainees and, like them, spending his free time in the common room. Except when he was not reading: because Slobodan Milošević is an ardent reader. He also likes taking a stroll in the courtyard. The prison in Scheveningen is on the waterfront, and he can hear the seagulls and breathe the salty air while watching the wind chase the clouds across the sky, big golden clouds straight out of Vermeer's paintings of Delft. Timothy McFadden says that now Milošević is nothing less than a model prisoner. He is cordial, speaks with everyone including the guards, doesn't seem to care about where a person comes from, and helps other inmates to learn English. And he praises Dragoljub Prcać when he is in charge of the kitchen, saying that he has never eaten so well before in his life.

But some of the old prestige is still attached to Milošević: curiously enough, Ademi addresses him as 'Mister President', although Milošević is no longer the President of Serbia, and even less of a president to someone like the Albanian Ademi who is a Croatian citizen.

Sitting next to Halilović are Miroslav Kvočka and Hazim Delić playing cards. If they want to, they can visit the library, which has some six hundred books, most of them in 'their' language. Or take a course in English or in painting. One detainee, Duško Tadić, has spent some time painting. There is a piano and a guitar in the common room, for anyone who likes to play music. Doctors and psychologists are at their service when needed, and even a massage can be ordered. But one of the most important privileges they enjoy is that they are allowed to smoke, both outside their rooms and in the common space as well. For the detainees, this is a blessing.

The day is grey, as it so often is in this part of Europe. A gentle rain is falling. Some of the younger men have gone out to the recreation area to play handball. They are no nationalists when it comes to sport; they all play together. One of them is the Bosnian Croat Mladen Naletilić Tuta, who is well over fifty. Before his extradition from Croatia, he was considered too ill to be put on a plane to The Hague. But he was put on a plane nevertheless, and once he was here in the Scheveningen detention unit his health miraculously improved. It seems that Scheveningen is beneficial to health, almost like a spa. Here, the detainees can spend the whole day out of their rooms, but if they prefer to stay in, to take a nap or read, the rooms are clean and big enough for their comfort. Each is equipped with a shower, a writing desk, a radio and a TV set. According to Tuta, compared to a prison in Zagreb, their quarters in Scheveningen are like rooms in a three-star hotel. The Dutch even call the prison the Orange Hotel – *Het Oranje Hotel* – not, however, because of the luxurious conditions, but because it is the building in which Dutch resistance fighters were imprisoned by the Nazis during the

Second World War. More than fifty years later it is not heroes but suspected war criminals from the Balkans who are living in this house.

Almost as if they really were on vacation in a beach hotel, the men are generally, with very rare exceptions, pleasant to each other. They do not quarrel or cause problems, says McFadden. Given that, in addition to belonging to different nationalities, they are also from different backgrounds and professions – former police officers, military men, teachers, politicians, taxi drivers, waiters and car mechanics – their harmony is an achievement. They comply with the house rules, and some of them are models of respect for law and order. McFadden himself is very protective of his detainees (not prisoners, of course) and makes sure that they all have what they need. Visitors may come every day; if they wish, they can stay all day. They need McFadden's approval to do so, but in a normal prison a visitor couldn't come more than once a month. They also get pocket money of a sort, two dollars a day, and for washing corridors and doing laundry they can earn five dollars a day, although there are not many candidates for that extra money. And they get a twenty-five-dollar telephone card each month. But perhaps the biggest sensation is the 'love room', in fact two rooms, where detainees can receive their wives and be together with them. Already, thanks to this facility, children have been born to the wives of both Zoran Žigić and Tihomir Blaškić.

Why do the detainees at the Scheveningen unit enjoy such extraordinary privileges? McFadden has a simple explanation: according to the law, these men are not guilty until it has been proven in court that they are, and therefore they and their families should suffer as little as possible. This is the reason, he says, that he hasn't even read the indictments against them: so that he can avoid being prejudiced. To him, they are not war criminals but ordinary people. However, McFadden's concern for the detainees, their rights and their life in comparative luxury – Scheveningen is certainly the most comfortable detention unit in Europe – is in such disproportion to the crimes they are suspected of having committed that it seems almost absurd, at least in the eyes of their victims. And it is hardly any consolation to the victims that the detainees won't enjoy similar privileges if they are actually sentenced and have to leave for other prisons in countries that have agreed with the United Nations to take them on, countries like Germany, Norway and Finland.

Something else that unites these men, besides food, language and sport, is that they are accused of having committed the worst war crimes in Europe since the Second World War. One would think that since they were at war with each other and might still be deadly enemies, it would be logical to place them on different floors according to their nationalities. But here Serbs and Croats and Bosnians, who for years fought each other, live happily together. And although each of them continues to stick to the political opinions that brought him to Scheveningen, they have obviously reached a compromise that enables them to live together – something that people back home can only dream about. 'When I came here, the first man who greeted me was Esad Landjo, a Muslim,' said Goran Jelisić, a Serb who specialised in executing Muslim prisoners from close range. 'He helped me. He told me about the rules and what was waiting for me in the court.' Back home Esad Landjo specialised in torturing Serbian prisoners.

The detainees not only help each other, they act together as well. When Milan Kovačević died and Slavko Dokmanović killed himself, they all sent messages of condolence to the families and flowers to the funerals. They also signed a petition together that was sent to the president of the Tribunal, asking for an improvement in the conditions in the detention centre, and they wrote an open letter to the media denying gossip about their alleged suffering from depression.

It is almost touching to see how much togetherness these men are capable of, how much solidarity there is among them, as if the air in Scheveningen can produce miracles not only for their physical wellbeing, but also for their souls. It is as if, once the electronic door of the prison closed behind them, they turned into different men. Suddenly there is no more of the nationalism that destroyed a whole country and took a quarter of a million lives.

How is it possible? Simo Zarić, accused of persecuting people of different – that is, Muslim and Croatian – origins (still, by all accounts Zarić is a small fry), is convinced that the spirit of unity among the detainees is very much what it used to be like in the old Yugoslav National Army. 'One has to adjust and survive,' he said.

The Yugoslav National Army? Indeed, this strikes me as an interesting comparison. The Yugoslav National Army was considered to be the best school of 'brotherhood and unity' (*bratstvo i jedinstvo*) in the old Yugoslavia, intended to uphold the widely propagated slogan of Tito as well as to keep together a country of six republics, three languages and three religions. All in vain, it seems. Because no matter how good the school was, brothers had no problem killing each other, and of unity there is not much left.

But in Scheveningen, Tito's Yugoslavia still seems to be alive. Just how peacefully the accused war criminals of different nationalities coexist is described in a poem written by Zarić himself. There, one can find lines like this:

> *It is not important what happened there*
> *but how it is now, here.*

Describing the life in the prison, the harmony and friendship of the prisoners, Zarić ends the poem with a message to people back home to follow their example!

This poem, called 'Truth About The Hague', became an informal anthem of the detainees in Scheveningen, accepted by everyone there. Goran Jelisić, who acts as a kind of spokesman for the group, told the public in the court (while attending the Landjo trial as a character witness) that men of different nationalities in their detention unit had achieved peace among themselves, but added that they had doubts as to whether people at home were capable of achieving the same thing. Together the detainees had come to the conclusion that 'the Tribunal has to contribute to the establishing of a lasting peace in Bosnia'.

In this conclusion, however, they apparently see no irony.

When night falls the men in Scheveningen withdraw into their cosy apartments, equipped with satellite dishes so that they can watch TV programmes in 'their' own language (a service no ordinary hotel room can offer) as well as coffee machines so that they can have a cup of coffee, just because they are used to it – to deprive them of this would mean denying them their rights. And before they fall asleep – with or without sleeping pills – none of them will give a thought to the paradox of Scheveningen: to the fact that, at the end of the day, it very much looks like Yugoslavia in miniature.

The Yugoslavia of 'brotherhood and unity' doesn't exist any longer, except in this very prison.

And the men who are most responsible for its falling apart, for the thousands upon thousands of victims of that war, are today living not only in unity like brothers, but in luxury. The life they lead in detention is the biggest anti-war demonstration one could imagine, except that it is being staged too late and those nice guys playing cards, cooking and watching TV are mocking the people back home who once took them so seriously. They ridicule those who followed their orders. They make fools of those who have lost their dear ones. They make all sacrifice meaningless.

But if the 'brotherhood and unity' among the sworn enemies of yesterday is indeed the epilogue of this war, one wonders: what was it all for? Looking at the merry boys in the Scheveningen detention unit the answer seems clear: for nothing.

ACKNOWLEDGEMENTS

I was lucky enough to get generous support from Hamburger Stiftung zur Förderung von Wissenschaft und Kultur, as well as from The Olaf Palme Centre in Stockholm. As a fellow of the Netherlands Institute for Advanced Study in the Humanities and Social Sciences (NIAS) from Wassenaar, I had excellent conditions for work and I was able to pay regular visits to the Tribunal in The Hague. I am especially grateful to NIAS fellow Willem Wagenaar, a professor of psychology at the University of Leiden, for many discussions that helped me to clarify my ideas. Ann Simpson was kind enough to edit my manuscript, and I would like to express my gratitude to her, too.

Mirko Klarin and Vjera Bogati from SENSA news agency helped me with all kinds of practical matters, and I could not have possibly written this book without their help. I also would like to thank my friend Tanja Petovar for insisting that I should write this book in the first place.

Needless to say, this book would probably look different without my husband Richard Swartz's wise suggestions.

Kultur Kontakt from Vienna helped me with travelling expenses, and I thank them for that.